Technology and the Resilience of Metropolitan Regions

THE URBAN AGENDA

Series Editor, Michael A. Pagano

Technology and the Resilience of Metropolitan Regions

EDITED BY MICHAEL A. PAGANO

University of Illinois at Chicago

PUBLISHED FOR THE
COLLEGE OF URBAN PLANNING
AND PUBLIC AFFAIRS (CUPPA),
UNIVERSITY OF ILLINOIS AT CHICAGO,
BY THE UNIVERSITY OF ILLINOIS PRESS
Urbana, Chicago, and Springfield

The College of Urban Planning and Public Affairs of the University of Illinois at Chicago and the University of Illinois Press gratefully acknowledge that publication of this book was assisted by a grant from the John D. and Catherine T. MacArthur Foundation.

© 2015 by the Board of Trustees
of the University of Illinois
All rights reserved
Manufactured in the United States of America
1 2 3 4 5 C P 5 4 3 2 1
∞ This book is printed on acid-free paper.

Cataloging Data available from the Library of Congress
ISBN 978-0-252-03916-4 (hardcover : alk.)
ISBN 978-0-252-08073-9 (paper : alk.)
ISBN 978-0-252-09714-0 (ebook)

Contents

Preface and Acknowledgments

The University of Illinois at Chicago (UIC) has hosted a forum on urban issues since 1995 when the first forum was convened under the auspices of the Great Cities Institute at UIC. The Winter Forum met annually until 2005, convening scholars, public intellectuals, policy makers, and elected officials from the Chicago region as well as from other parts of the country. Starting in 2005, UIC in partnership with the City of Chicago hosted the Richard J. Daley Urban Forum annually for six years. This forum was designed from its beginnings as a collaboration aimed at convening key public, private, and nonprofit leaders in an academic arena to discuss, analyze, and propose pragmatic and innovative solutions to enhance the lives of city dwellers around the globe.

In 2012, UIC chancellor Paula Allen-Meares revitalized the UIC annual conference on urban issues, titling it the UIC Urban Forum, and charging it with the responsibility of bringing together policy makers, academics, public intellectuals, students, community activists, and citizens to discuss, debate, and recommend policy action to the pressing and intractable challenges of cities and metropolitan regions. The activities of the UIC Urban Forum are directed toward two major goals: staging a major annual event to advance a national and global dialogue about the urban future; and disseminating policy options, recommendations, and best practices.

PARTNERSHIP AND COLLABORATION

The UIC Urban Forum works in collaboration with a multiplicity of partners, including foundations, the nonprofit community, governments, the corporate sector, and the media. The partners of the 2013 UIC Urban Forum included the Chicago Community Trust, the John D. and Catherine T. Mac-Arthur Foundation, Abbott, Cerner, Takeda, Walgreen's, UIC's College of Urban Planning and Public Affairs, and UIC's Institute for Policy and Civic Engagement, whose financial support was instrumental in the success of the forum. The MacArthur grant was provided as a subvention in support of underwriting the costs of this publication and disseminating the book.

The UIC Urban Forum also partnered with the local National Public Radio affiliate, WBEZ, which supplied moderators for the morning panels. The UIC Urban Forum expresses its profound gratitude to Vanessa Harris, WBEZ's director of marketing, and Alison Scholly, chief operating officer. Their support and assistance in strengthening the reach of the forum's impact is deeply appreciated.

The UIC Urban Forum also operates in partnership with the University of Illinois Press. The edited white papers from the UIC Urban Forum are presented in a series called the Urban Agenda. Each annual volume is designed to publish the conference's proceedings as well as a synopsis of the panel "conversations with local officials" from the conference. This volume is the second installment of the partnership. I am indebted to the director of the University of Illinois Press, Willis Regier, whose support and oversight of the publication process make him an indispensable and discerning partner in the program.

Finally, the UIC Urban Forum's primary internal partner is the UIC College of Urban Planning and Public Affairs (CUPPA). The project director of the UIC Urban Forum is the dean of the college, and the executive committee consists of CUPPA's director of the Great Cities Institute and a delegate from the chancellor's office.

THE 2013 UIC URBAN FORUM

The theme of the 2013 UIC Urban Forum was Technology and the Resilience of Metropolitan Regions, and the invitation to attend the event stated the following: "People and institutions engage in the public square and the private marketplace for the purpose of promoting commerce and growth, improving residents' health and the quality of life in neighborhoods and cities, and creating institutions to promote democratic governance. These interactions are shaped by rapidly emerging technologies and access to those technologies by individuals and institutions. Today, the capacities of institutions, communities, and societies to govern collectively and ensure a sustainable and acceptable quality of life for metropolitan regions are increasingly challenged. The shape and direction of metropolitan growth and development depends on access to appropriate technology that is scaled and informed by the individual, household and community needs of the metropolitan region."

The 2013 event was cochaired by Cook County Board president Toni Preckwinkle and Chancellor Paula Allen-Meares of UIC. The daylong event was held on December 5, 2013, beginning with two panels in the morning moderated by WBEZ news reporters. The four afternoon panels were organized around the themes of the four white papers. At the opening of the day's event, Cook County Board president Toni Preckwinkle keynoted the event by reminding the audience that a critical component to economic growth and development in the modern era requires that open data and mobile technologies be made accessible to all and that government efficiency and effectiveness must be enhanced by better analyzing "big data." A metropolitan region's future depends on how well and how effectively governments and the private sector can harness the productive promises of technology.

The 2013 UIC Urban Forum was organized by an executive committee that chose the theme of the conference, a committee of UIC scholars that identified the white papers and the authors, an external advisory board that recommended participants for the morning panels, and an operations committee responsible for organizing and planning the conference. The executive committee, which I chaired, included the UIC Great Cities Institute director Teresa Córdova, and UIC dean of education, Vicki Chou. The UIC Committee of Academic Advisors included Karen Mossberger and Howard Wial.

The external board of advisors included Bruce Katz (vice president of the Brookings Institution and director of the Metropolitan Policy Program), Henry Cisneros (former HUD secretary and mayor of San Antonio; founder and chairman, CityView), Lee Fisher (president and CEO of CEOs for Cities), Clarence Anthony (executive director of the National League of Cities), Terry Mazany (president of the Chicago Community Trust), MarySue Barrett (president of the Metropolitan Planning Council), Randy Blankenhorn (executive director of the Chicago Metropolitan Agency for Planning), Jeffery Malehorn (president of World Business Chicago), Karen Freeman-Wilson (mayor of Gary), Rahm Emanuel (mayor of Chicago), Toni Preckwinkle (chairman, Cook County Board of Commissioners) and Michael Coleman (mayor of Columbus).

Participants on the panels included the following:

- Brian Kelly, president, Payer and Provider Solutions, Quintiles
- John Tolva, former chief technology officer, City of Chicago
- Susana Vasquez, executive director, Local Incentives Support Corporation

- Tim Wisniewski, director of civic technology, City of Philadelphia
- Natalie Moore, reporter, WBEZ, Chicago Public Radio
- Mark Harris, president and CEO, Illinois Science and Technology Coalition
- Jeffery Malehorn, president and CEO, World Business Chicago
- Theresa E. Mintle, president and CEO, Chicagoland Chamber of Commerce
- Ted Smith, director of economic growth and innovation, City of Louisville
- Niala Boodhoo, host, *Afternoon Shift*, WBEZ, Chicago Public Radio
- Scott Bernstein, president and cofounder, the Center for Neighborhood Technology
- Jane E. Fountain, professor of political science and public policy, adjunct professor of computer science, University of Massachusetts, Amherst
- Jon Gant, professor, University of Illinois Urbana-Champaign
- Daniel X. O'Neil, executive director, SmartChicago Collaborative
- John Hendren, English correspondent, Al Jazeera
- Don Bisbee, senior vice president, Cerner DeviceWorks
- Bénédicte Callan, clinical professor, Arizona State University College for Health Solutions
- Jerry A. Krishnan, professor of medicine and public health, associate vice president for population health sciences, University of Illinois College of Medicine at Chicago
- Julio Silva, chief medical information officer, Rush University Medical Center
- Michelle Stohlmeyer Russell, partner and manager, Boston Consulting Group
- Randy Blankenhorn, executive director, Chicago Metropolitan Agency for Planning
- Herman Brewer, bureau chief, Cook County Bureau of Economic Development
- Scott Miller, owner and president, the Innovation Machine
- Howard Wial, executive director, Center for Urban Economic Development, University of Illinois at Chicago
- Brian Fabes, CEO, Civic Consulting Alliance
- Mary Rose Hennessy, founder and executive director, University of Illinois Business and Industry Services
- Sandee Kastrul, cofounder and president, i.c.stars

- Alfred Tatum, interim dean of the College of Education, University of Illinois at Chicago
- Darrell M. West, vice president and director of governance studies, Brookings Institution
- Steve Koch, deputy mayor, City of Chicago

Finally, I wish to acknowledge the following persons who met regularly for over six months to ensure the smooth operating success of the 2013 UIC Urban Forum. Jenny Sweeny, whose oversight of the event and involvement in the minutiae of ensuring an outstanding conference, deserves a heartfelt thanks from all of us. Without her dedication and supervision, the conference would not have been nearly as successful as it was. Jennifer Woodard, in the UIC Office of the Vice President for Research, was extraordinarily successful in securing the participation of many panelists; a deep debt of gratitude is owed her. Others who were instrumental in the success of the event include Darcy Evon and Rona Heifetz, who undertook the advancement work of the project, Bill Burton from the UIC Office of External Affairs, Sarah Falconer, Stephanie Truchan, and Miryam Miza, who as graduate assistants performed heroically on all assigned tasks, and the team from Jasculca-Terman Associates, especially Kristi Sebestyen, Maureen Meehan, Carly Olsman, Bailey Vance, and Dan Regan, whose contributions cannot be underestimated.

The editorial assistance and manuscript supervision by Stephanie Truchan, who was responsible for both the book-production process and for writing the summary of the panelists' conversations ("Plugged In" in part 3), were undertaken superbly. Stephanie deserves the gratitude of everyone whose contributions appear in this book.

The three hundred registrants of the one-day conference were challenged to understand, embrace, and carefully deploy the rapidly changing technology that has become indispensable to human life in the modern era. Technology's adaptation to ensure better political participation and governance, to reach inaccessible populations to provide health care, to provide opportunities for economic growth and workforce development, must be better understood and used to enhance the human condition. The annual UIC Urban Forum will continue to offer thoughtful conferences on critical urban issues in a venue to which all of the world's citizens are invited.

Michael A. Pagano

Project Director, 2013 UIC Urban Forum

Dean, UIC College of Urban Planning and Public Affairs

Chicago, March 2014

PART ONE
OVERVIEW

Toward Connected, Innovative, and Resilient Metro Regions

KAREN MOSSBERGER, CHEN-YU KAO,

AND KUANG-TING TAI

ARIZONA STATE UNIVERSITY

Why should policymakers care about information technology use in their regions? Quite simply, because today information technology is fundamentally transforming the way in which we do nearly everything. These changes are important for the capacities and opportunities of individual residents, and for the development, quality of life, and resilience of communities.

For individuals, Internet use is necessary to participate fully in society, for access to information on jobs, government services, and health care, for civic engagement, and for economic opportunity.[1] Think about how we apply for jobs today, file our taxes, compare prices, look for a new apartment, check on our children's homework and grades, and navigate our way around. Information and communication online are so essential that the United Nations has called Internet access a human right.[2]

Yet, nationally, and in the city of Chicago, about 30 percent of the population in 2013 did not have broadband at home—they did not have regular and effective access to the Internet.[3] Approximately 15 percent of Chicago residents (and 15% nationally) did not use the Internet at all.

This is a public policy concern for many reasons, including the public benefits that can be generated from technology use, for innovation and community resilience, as well as for social equity. Local governments are critical actors in realizing these policy goals, and the interconnected fabric of metropolitan regions makes it important to examine these issues at that scale.

Information technology use matters for what economists call public goods, as the benefits of Internet use are not confined to the individuals who use the technology, but affect communities as a whole. Broadband, or high-speed

Internet, makes possible innovative uses in health, education, economic development, energy and environmental management, mass transit, public safety and emergency management, government service delivery, political participation, and many other areas important to the development and quality of life in communities. The public-goods characteristic of broadband has inspired the creation of wide-ranging initiatives that cross policy areas, such as the FCC's plan for national broadband in the United States and the European Commissions' *Digital Agenda for Europe*.[4] Yet it is local governments that have substantial responsibility in many of these policy areas in the United States and that have the potential for important leadership on technology use.

Major cities and their metropolitan regions are the engines of the national economy.[5] They are population centers with enormous social impact for the nation as a whole. Today two-thirds of Americans live in the top one hundred metropolitan areas, which cover 12 percent of land space but produce 75 percent of national gross domestic product (GDP).[6] These metropolitan regions are defined by a common labor market and commuting patterns,[7] and the actions of neighboring communities easily spill across boundaries. Metro areas are connected through multiple interactions and networks, which can be enhanced through information technology use.

To introduce the contributions in this book, we begin by discussing the role of digital technology for local and metropolitan innovation, public goods, and resilience. While the individual chapters examine the significance of technology in several critical areas—workforce development, advanced manufacturing, health, and e-government—there is a need to frame these policy areas in a more general context, including theories of urban development and the metropolitan institutional environment. Next, we examine the presence of neighborhood and metropolitan disparities in technology use that present challenges for realizing these public policy goals, considering actions to foster better public policy.

METROPOLITAN INNOVATION AND SOCIAL BENEFITS

Public and private efforts alike envision cities and their urban regions as incubators for technological innovation across policy areas. Google is installing superfast gigabit broadband networks in Kansas City, Kansas, and Kansas City, Missouri, and more recently, Austin, Texas, and Provo, Utah.[8] The White House Office of Science and Technology Policy launched US Ignite in partnership with six city-regions that agreed to experiment with applications for gigabit broadband with the goals of transforming "how we receive healthcare, educate our children, keep our communities safe, become more energy efficient, train our employees, and manufacture goods."[9] World-wide, technology firms such as Cisco and IBM have partnered with local governments for "smart city" solutions, including powering electrical grids, managing transportation systems, protecting public safety, and promoting environmental sustainability.[10]

Social and economic innovations are most likely to occur in dense and diverse metropolitan areas, with their specialized labor markets, intense activity, knowledge spillovers across firms, larger and more specialized governments, and wealth of cultural and research institutions.[11] Through their density and scale, "cities concentrate, accelerate, and diversify social and economic activity."[12] Cities and their metropolitan regions can be viewed as an "innovation ecosystem empowering the collective intelligence and co-creation capabilities of user/citizen communities for designing innovative living and working scenarios." The application of information and communication technologies can positively affect this ecosystem.[13]

Broadband use in communities can stimulate economic development.[14] Information technology applications across sectors and in a variety of industries drive productivity and growth.[15] In urban areas, firms are more likely to adopt advanced technologies and employ more complex uses of the Internet that lead to greater productivity and economic growth. In contrast, rural firms tend to use the Internet in basic ways, such as for email or web browsing.[16] The thicker labor markets in metro areas facilitate more knowledge spillovers across firms, and the cost of innovation using the Internet is lower because firms can draw upon existing talent and skills rather than developing them internally.[17] The development of advanced manufacturing technologies discussed by Howard Wial in this book is one example.

Economic theories of urban leadership in technology use point to the skills of the workforce for using technology as an important factor in urban innovation. Wage growth associated with Internet use is disproportionately concentrated in metropolitan areas, indicating higher returns to skill.[18] Workforce development policies, however, are often instruments for addressing both skill and income disparities, and there is evidence that Internet use matters for individual wages as well. Longitudinal data demonstrates that Internet use at home and on the job leads to higher wages, likely because home Internet use signals useful skills.[19] Other research shows that Internet use at work results in higher wages even for workers with a high school education or less.[20] These findings suggest that workforce development should address technology skills for disadvantaged workers as well as for a competitive edge in attracting or developing businesses with more knowledge-intensive occupations. Darrell West examines technology and workforce development in metro regions in his contribution to this book.

Concentrating the nation's population, as well as medical and research institutions, metropolitan areas are important test beds for health care reforms. These include emerging practices that empower individuals with more information and tools for managing their health, as described by Bénédicte Callan in this book.

As Jane Fountain discusses in her contribution, information technology also makes possible innovations for government, including more convenient, efficient, and around-the-clock access to services and information. Additionally, however, governments are experimenting with open-data portals, social media, and online town hall meetings that promise opportunities for greater transparency and dialogue on public issues.[21] Local governments have long been regarded as schools for democracy where face-to-face participation is most likely to occur,[22] and so the development of e-government at the local level has important potential for fostering civic participation, as well as trust and confidence in government.[23] Large cities have traditionally been pioneers in e-government use,[24] with more professionalization as well as greater scale.

Although the contributions in this book focus on advanced manufacturing, workforce development, health, and e-government, there are many other ways in which digital technologies can improve urban services and quality of life. Mass transit and energy conservation are just two examples of information technology applications with particular resonance for cities and metropolitan areas.

Exploiting positioning sensors and computing techniques, investment in public transportation has shifted from traditional infrastructure to IT-based service improvements, which emphasize pre-trip information, on-board information, smart cards, and other convenient processes.[25] "Big data" can be harnessed for better modeling of traffic flows and planning, and real-time information on traffic and parking is available in many cities.[26] Through the use of the computing abilities of information technology, city governments can make optimum use of existing infrastructure in order to reduce consumption of fossil fuels and achieve significant greenhouse gas emissions reduction.[27] The City of Pleasanton, California, for example, uses a traffic camera system to identify and differentiate between cars and bicycles so that it can adjust the timing of the traffic light for cars or bicycles to cross a busy intersection. This helps reduce car idling, unnecessary fossil fuel consumption, and greenhouse gas emissions.[28]

Energy information systems (EISs) have been used in cities to measure energy usage performance and are viewed as a promising technology to reduce energy use in buildings.[29] Smart meters are EIS applications that provide consumers with detailed and real-time energy consumption information, but also link this information directly to the utility provider, who can apply dynamic pricing based on the use of energy in peak and nonpeak hours. Smart meters increase consumers' awareness of energy usage and have the potential to change energy use behaviors, and help achieve energy saving in a city as a whole. For example, Pacific Gas and Electric tested dynamic pricing in Bakersfield, California, on 2,300 homes under this system. The result showed there was as much as a 13 percent decrease in peak-hour energy usage.[30]

Technology can also be used for "crowdsourcing" and bottom-up processes of problem solving. In cities across the globe, "Living Labs" present challenges faced by cities and submitted by local governments, inviting citizens and organizations to develop solutions.[31] Digital technologies can power a number of improvements for metropolitan areas through their ability to transmit information and provide new opportunities for communication and participation.

METROPOLITAN RESILIENCE

The same density, scale, and complexity of metropolitan regions that fosters innovation and impact can also create vulnerability to environmental hazards, natural disasters, public safety threats, economic shocks, and other disruptions. Natural disasters such as Hurricane Katrina and Superstorm Sandy, along with the tragedy of the World Trade Center, have placed concerns about metropolitan resilience on urban agendas. A resilient system is defined by its several features—its ability to absorb change and disturbance; the persistence of systems while retaining its basic functions and structure;[32] and the ability to survive, adapt, and transform itself.[33] Not just concerned with preventing disturbances, resilience also involves adaptation to change.[34]

Some concepts have been applied by scholars to define the measurable aspects of resilient cities. These concepts include recovery, connectivity, social capital, adaptability, robustness, flexibility, and transformability.[35] Information technology is a critical resource for the establishment and enhancement of these aspects of resilience in an urban system.[36]

Information is crucial. An urban system must have the capacity to sense incremental and major changes in the environment. It must then further use the information gathered to learn from past experience, to experiment with possible alternative actions, and to anticipate the future.[37]

Technology is also important for connectivity.[38] For example, Deborah Wallace and Rodrick Wallace conclude that the social networks and interconnections between urban neighborhoods are the basis of metropolitan resilience.[39] Information technology also helps promote interconnectivity within and between metropolitan areas.[40] Examples of IT usage in enhancing interconnectivity and urban resilience can be found in research on disaster management. These studies indicate that the use of online social media in crisis events and in disasters can facilitate public participation in recovery efforts and communication during the response. For example, Leysia Palen studies how local residents used online social media to acquire, disseminate, and communicate information in the 2007 Southern California wildfires.[41] She also indicates the insufficiency of traditional media and official channels in providing real-time information. Sophia Liu et al. also describe the use of the online photo-sharing website Flickr in disaster preparation, warning, response, and recovery efforts, and conclude that this use of information technology has increased the interconnectivity of citizens and has fostered grassroots activities which are essential for metropolitan disaster resilience.[42] Information technologies contribute to the adaptability and flexibility of urban systems by connecting decentralized and distributed resources across the region, by making information available to residents and businesses, and providing networks for communication.

INCLUSION IS NEEDED FOR INNOVATION AND RESILIENCE

Internet use has network externalities—that is, the social benefits of technology increase with widespread use and inclusive networks. Regions that have lower rates of Internet use are constrained in a number of ways—in the skills within the local workforce, for example, in the ability of local governments to deliver services online more efficiently and effectively, or in the capacity of local hospitals to promote preventive care through patient information. Low rates of broadband adoption at home affect the ability of school districts to transform K–12 education through methods like flipped classrooms and to involve parents on a more continuous basis through school portals. Neighborhoods with few residents online are likely to suffer disproportionately during crises. As Hurricane Katrina demonstrated, low-income neighborhoods often have fewer resources to cope with disasters, anyway; a lack of connectivity makes them even more vulnerable. In general, local institutions can't fully move into the digital age when the populations they serve are offline or only tenuously connected to the Internet.

For residents, digital citizenship, or the ability to participate in society online, requires both regular access to the Internet and the skills to use it.[43] One way in which to measure the quality of access and skills that individuals have is to examine the range of activities they are able to engage in online. This is especially true for what Eszter Hargittai has called human capital–enhancing activities online—for jobs, finances, education, health care, political participation, and civic engagement.[44] These are more demanding activities requiring some knowledge about how to search for and use information that Internet users engage in with greater experience and higher levels of education.[45] These are exactly the goals of policies such as the National Broadband Plan.[46] Forms of access matter, as broadband adoption at home (or the combination of broadband and mobile phones) is significantly associated with a greater range of activities online, controlling for other factors.[47]

As mobile technology proliferates, and is embraced at high rates by African Americans and Latinos, assumptions abound about the disappearance of the "digital divide." According to the Pew Internet and American Life Project, nationally 74 percent of African American cell phone users and 68 percent of Latino cell phone users access the Internet on their smartphones, in contrast with 59 percent of non-Hispanic whites.[48] A small percentage of the population goes online, however, primarily through mobile phones, without broadband at home. This group is predominantly African American and Latino, low-income, less-educated, and young.[49] It accounted for 9 percent of African Americans and 15 percent of Latinos in Chicago in 2013.[50] They enjoy some of the benefits of technology, but according to research, mobile-only Internet users do less online and have fewer technology skills.[51] So, while the spread of mobile phones is changing how and where individuals use the Internet, broadband at home is still an important indicator to track for comparing technology adoption and disparities. Fully connected Internet users are those who have multiple devices, combining the continual access and mobility of smart phones and the functionality of larger screens and keyboards on laptops and personal computers.

Cities and Metros across the Nation

Technology use varies substantially between cities and regions, according to estimates for Internet use and broadband use for the fifty largest cities and their suburban areas based on the 2009 Current Population Survey, conducted by the U.S. Bureau of the Census.[52] Broadband adoption at home ranged between 39 percent in Buffalo and 83 percent in Seattle. Other cities at the top of the list have an IT industry presence and highly educated populations, such as Portland, Oregon, San Francisco, and San Jose. Those at the bottom of the list included places with substantial poverty and disinvestment, such as Cleveland, Detroit, and Rochester, New York, or cities with high proportions of Latinos, such as Los Angeles, San Antonio, and Miami. But, while African Americans and Latinos had lower rates of Internet use or broadband adoption than non-Hispanic whites in all cities, the disparities were smaller in places where there was a high percentage of the population as a whole online. In this case, traditionally disadvantaged groups were more likely to be digital citizens when there was a technology-rich environment overall.[53]

Comparing broadband adoption and Internet use estimates for central cities and suburbs shows that while cities generally lagged behind their suburbs, the pair tended to place similarly in the rankings. Scholars have argued that central-city and suburban economic fortunes are closely linked by the common regional economy, and this seems to be true for the most part for Internet use in metropolitan areas.[54] Yet, glaring exceptions appeared where there were wider gaps in technology use between city and suburban rankings. For example, Milwaukee, Denver, and Rochester's center cities ranked low in Internet use, yet their suburban regions were in the top ten. The Milwaukee metropolitan area is one of the most racially segregated in the United States, and Denver has a high percentage of Latinos.[55] Regional information technology disparities clearly reflect other social inequalities in metropolitan areas.

The estimates described above, based on the 2009 Current Population Survey, did not differentiate between suburban jurisdictions within regions. In recent decades, suburban poverty has grown, and it varies across jurisdictions within metropolitan areas.[56] It is an oversimplification to compare only city and suburban disparities, as some poor suburbs clearly have needs for greater digital inclusion as well, and some other survey data show commonalities between central cities and some of their suburbs. Using a 2012 survey of Cuyahoga County residents, Tolbert and Mossberger estimated Internet use and activities online across the different municipalities in Cuyahoga County, Ohio. Cleveland and its inner rings suburbs were disadvantaged in Internet use in most respects, except for higher rates of mobile access.[57] Extending this analysis for individual municipalities showed that estimated home broadband adoption varied from 50 percent in Warrensville, 53 percent in East Cleveland, and 54 percent in Cleveland, to 93 percent in Pepper Pike, an affluent eastern suburb.[58] Clearly suburban regions are not homogenous in terms of technology use, and these gaps may affect the capacity of low-income suburban communities for effective delivery of government services, economic development, and education.

Chicago Neighborhoods: Place Matters

It is in Chicago, which falls midway in the national city rankings and which has rates of Internet use near national averages, that we can see place-based patterns of disparities in urban neighborhoods, as well. Research on the effects of concentrated poverty and segregation has demonstrated what the Brookings Institution has called the "double burden" of being poor and living in a high-poverty neighborhood.[59] Spatial concentration of poverty is associated with disparities in health,[60] education,[61] labor markets,[62] collective efficacy,[63] and political participation.[64] Use of multilevel models to analyze national data indicate that beyond individual characteristics, residence in low-income areas also diminishes the likelihood of Internet use, and similar analyses show the impact of neighborhood segregation and poverty in Chicago for home broadband adoption.[65]

Paradoxically, while Internet use could help transcend the constraints faced by residents in low-income neighborhoods, technology inequalities are shaped by the same geography of poverty. By comparing Internet use and activities online in the most-connected and least-connected Chicago community areas, the impact of these disparities is readily apparent. The tables in this chapter give 2013 estimates for Internet use in Chicago's neighborhoods, for the most-connected community areas (table 1) and the least-connected (see table 2).[66]

In the highest-ranked Chicago neighborhoods listed in table 1, Internet use is almost universal, and approximately nine out of ten residents have broadband at home. These high-ranked neighborhoods are in affluent or solidly middle-class areas, mostly on the north side of the city (with the exception of Beverly). Residents of these community areas are much more likely to perform most activities online; the exception is job searching, which lies around the city average in most of these neighborhoods. In these connected neighborhoods, a higher percentage of residents go online to get information on health, transit, government, and politics, and to take a class online.

In neighborhoods where a low percentage of the population has broadband at home or uses the Internet anywhere, it is not surprising that smaller percentages of residents are engaged in all of these activities online (table 2). What is striking, however, is how few people access information online, and the subsequent impact for individual opportunity and community outcomes in these neighborhoods. It is sobering to realize that only about half of residents in these neighborhoods look up health information online (the most common activity) and only one-third or less search for jobs online in each of

Table 1. Internet Use and Online Activities for Highest-Ranked Chicago Community Areas, 2013

Broadband Use Highest-Ranked Area (%)	Internet Use Percentage	Health Info. Percentage	Job Search Percentage	Online Class Percentage
O'Hare (91)	98	91	48	55
Near West Side (90)	98	85	70	60
Lincoln Park (90)	98	86	52	51
Beverly (89)	98	86	54	50
Lake View (89)	98	86	51	50
North Center (89)	98	85	51	49
City Average (70)	84	74	58	45

Broadband Use Highest-Ranked Area (%)	Transportation Info. Percentage	E-Govt. Info. Percentage	Chicago Govt. Website Percentage	Politics Info. Percentage
O'Hare (91)	84	83	75	84
Near West Side (90)	84	79	73	80
Lincoln Park (90)	82	79	73	80
Beverly (89)	75	76	73	75
Lake View (89)	80	78	72	78
North Center (89)	78	78	77	76
City Average (70)	66	61	58	60

Source: Multilevel models from data in Karen Mossberger, Caroline J. Tolbert, and Christopher Anderson, "Measuring Change in Internet Use and Broadband Adoption: Comparing BTOP Smart Communities and Other Chicago Neighborhoods [Updated 2014]," April 2014.

Table 2. Internet Use and Online Activities for Lowest-Ranked Chicago Community Areas, 2013

Broadband Use Lowest-Ranked Area (%)	Internet Use Percentage	Health Info. Percentage	Job Search Percentage	Online Class Percentage
West Garfield Park (39)	63	49	30	17
Burnside (39)	57	50	24	17
Brighton Park (40)	61	49	25	17
Gage Park (42)	64	51	28	16
South Lawndale (43)	62	53	33	17
East Side (43)	61	52	24	15
City Average (70)	84	74	58	45

Broadband Use Lowest-Ranked Area (%)	Transportation Info. Percentage	E-Govt. Info. Percentage	Chicago Govt. Website Percentage	Politics Info. Percentage
West Garfield Park (39)	45	36	41	35
Burnside (39)	36	40	40	38
Brighton Park (40)	36	32	37	26
Gage Park (42)	34	31	36	25
South Lawndale (43)	34	33	36	27
East Side (43)	35	35	36	30
City Average (70)	66	61	58	60

Source: Multilevel models from data in Karen Mossberger, Caroline J. Tolbert and Christopher Anderson, "Measuring Change in Internet Use and Broadband Adoption: Comparing BTOP Smart Communities and Other Chicago Neighborhoods [Updated 2014]," April 2014.

these community areas. While there is some variation across the community areas, all trail the city averages by at least 20 percentage points in health, 25 percentage points in job search, 28 percentage points in online classes, 21 percentage points in transportation and government information, 18 percentage points in use of the city website, and 22 percentage points in political information. There are many "less-connected" Internet users in these neighborhoods, who go online at least occasionally, but do not have broadband at home.[67] For example, Internet use (anywhere) is estimated to be at least 20 percentage points higher than broadband at home in Brighton Park and Gage Park. In the more affluent neighborhoods that are highly connected, the differences between broadband adoption at home and Internet use anywhere is less than 10 percentage points. This indicates that many residents of poor neighborhoods recognize a need to use the Internet, but that affordability and other barriers prevent them from gaining home access.[68]

TOWARD A MODEL OF METROPOLITAN TECHNOLOGY CAPACITY

While the Internet is a vital resource for cities and metropolitan regions for a variety of reasons—for innovation, social benefits, and resilience—there is substantial inequality in the United States in Internet use across cities and metropolitan areas, and within them.

As complex systems, metro regions have markets, governments, and civic institutions that vary in their ability to take advantage of innovation or to adapt and thrive in the face of social, economic, and technological change. The regional character of the U.S. economy makes it more like a league of nations rather than a single national system, and federalism decentralizes public policies and governance, as well.[69] Authority is often fragmented across hundreds of municipalities and special districts and shared with state and federal agencies. This raises questions about the potential for diverse regions to take advantage of information technology—to build widespread, innovative, adaptive, and inclusive networks of use embracing businesses, governments, community anchor institutions, and residents.

What can be done to address technology inclusion in metropolitan areas? Actions undertaken by neighborhoods and cities can change outcomes. Research on the Smart Communities program in Chicago[70] indicates that between 2008 and 2013, Internet use, broadband at home, and Internet use for information on jobs, health, and transportation experienced a statistically significant increase in participating neighborhoods, in comparison with other

Chicago community areas.[71] Surveys of program participants and interviews with community organizations also provide further evidence of change in these communities.[72]

Yet, individual neighborhood programs may have insufficient scale without additional support, and cities with the highest need often have the fewest resources to promote digital inclusion in their schools, libraries, and community centers. Because the private sector provides most Internet services, the affordability of home broadband access is a need that has not been well-addressed by public policy. Can collaboration at a regional scale provide a stronger basis for policy leadership than the efforts of individual cities?

Bruce Katz and Jennifer Bradley have argued that metros are the most likely to offer solutions to many policy problems, and regional efforts potentially have more power and scale.[73] For example, in Northeast Ohio, One Community has been a vehicle for addressing high-speed infrastructure, cutting-edge applications in institutions such as the Cleveland Clinic and Case Western University, alongside digital inclusion programs that bring together partners such as neighborhood groups and county government.[74] The Google Fiber initiative is also an example of regional collaboration, between Kansas City, Kansas, and Kansas City, Missouri. Google is providing the gigabit broadband, but local governments and nonprofit organizations are partners who will be important for determining the extent to which this project results in greater inclusion. Just as local governments have pooled their resources to purchase insurance or other goods at favorable prices, there could be a metropolitan partnership to work with broadband providers or to form a public-private partnership for innovative broadband use, affordable high-speed broadband, and training.

Regional organizations can also convene and coordinate existing efforts, to collaborate with the private sector and nonprofits, or to provide a voice for change at other levels of government. Programs such as Internet Essentials and Connect2Compete offer discounted broadband for households with children enrolled in free or reduced-price school lunch programs, but there are many eligible households not reached. A coordinated regional effort could be more effective than a patchwork of initiatives in individual communities. The Federal Communications Commission is debating changes to the Lifeline program, which now provides subsidies for phone service for low-income individuals but could support broadband access in the future. Local interests could be more effectively represented by regional coalitions at the federal level, working with state agencies that also have a role in determining how the Lifeline program is implemented. Regional cooperation around broadband issues could also foster learning across programs and jurisdictions, about digital inclusion programs, or emerging practices for economic development, education, and more.

Regions are integrally interconnected—through their labor markets, economic activity, and costs and benefits that spill over across municipal and other jurisdictional boundaries. Residents access services from different governments in the region, especially in the Chicago area, which is one of the most fragmented and complex, with many municipalities, townships, special districts, and counties.[75] Information technology can provide a basis for innovation in firms and effective, transparent, and accountable government. The regional scale is an ideal arena for learning across sectors, to take advantage of experimentation across the many businesses, governments and nonprofit organizations that populate a metropolitan area. A resilient region is one that has rapid information flows and connectivity to promote efforts reaching across residents, sectors, and communities. An agenda for inclusion is also an investment in the human capital of the region—for greater access for all to resources for education, health, economic opportunity, and civic participation. As is evident in high-performing metro areas, where a high proportion of the population is online, traditionally disadvantaged groups are more likely to be fully connected, as well.[76] In Chicagoland and in other regions, there is good reason for collective action at the metropolitan scale to promote a vision of a connected region—one that is innovative, resilient, and inclusive.

Notes

We gratefully acknowledge the contributions that others have made to this chapter, especially Caroline Tolbert of the University of Iowa (on multiple projects) and William Franko of Auburn University for our joint work on digital cities, cited here. The Chicago research was supported by the John D. and Catherine T. MacArthur Foundation, Partnership for a Connected Illinois, and Institute for Policy and Civic Engagement at the University of Illinois at Chicago. The Cuyahoga County research was funded by One Community.

1. Karen Mossberger, Caroline J. Tolbert, and Ramona S. McNeal, *Digital Citizenship: The Internet, Society and Participation* (Cambridge, Mass.: MIT Press, 2008).

2. David Kravet, "U.N. Report Declares Internet Access a Human Right," 2011, accessed February 12, 2014, www.wired.com.

3. National Telecommunications and Information Administration, 2013, "Household Broadband Adoption Climbs to 72.4%," accessed February 12, 2014, www.ntia.doc .gov; Karen Mossberger, Caroline J. Tolbert, and Christopher Anderson, "Measuring

Change in Internet Use and Broadband Adoption: Comparing BTOP Smart Communities and Other Chicago Neighborhoods [Updated 2014]," accessed October 15, 2014, https://cpi.asu.edu, 17.

4. FCC, *Connecting America: The National Broadband Plan*, Washington, D.C.: Federal Communications Commission, 2010, accessed February 12, 2014, www.broadband .gov; European Commission, *A Digital Agenda for Europe*, European Commission, 2010, accessed February 12, 2014, http://eur-lex.europa.eu.

5. Bruce Katz and Jennifer Bradley, *The Metropolitan Revolution: How Cities and Metros Are Fixing Our Broken Politics and Fragile Economy* (Washington, D.C.: Brookings Institution Press, 2013); Larry C. Ledebur and William R. Barnes, *The New Regional Economies* (London: Sage Publications, 1998); Edward Glaser, *Triumph of the City: How Our Greatest Invention Makes Us Richer, Smarter, Greener, Healthier and Happier* (New York: Penguin, 2011).

6. Katz and Bradley, *Metropolitan Revolution*.

7. Ibid.

8. See https://fiber.google.com/about/.

9. US Ignite, *What Is US Ignite?*, 2013, accessed February 12, 2014, http://us-ignite .org.

10. Gordon Falconer and Shane Mitchell, *Smart City Framework: A Systematic Process for Enabling Smart+Connected Communities*, Cisco Internet Business Solutions Group, 2012, accessed February 12, 2014, www.cisco.com.

11. Chris Forman, Avi Goldfarb, and Shane Greenstein, *Technology Adoption In and Out of Major Urban Areas: When Do Internal Firm Resources Matter Most?*, National Bureau of Economic Research, 2005, accessed February 12, 2014, www .nber.org; Chris Forman, Avi Goldfarb, and Shane Greenstein, "Understanding the Inputs into Innovation: Do Cities Substitute for Internal Firm Resources?," *Journal of Economics and Management Strategy* 17, no. 2 (2008): 205–316; *The Internet and Local Wages: Convergence or Divergence?*, National Bureau of Economic Research, 2009, accessed February 12, 2014, www.nber.org; Edward Glaeser, *Triumph of the City: How Our Greatest Invention Makes Us Richer, Smarter, Greener, Healthier and Happier* (New York: Penguin, 2011), 247.

12. Luís M. A. Bettencourt and Geoffrey B. West, "Bigger Cities Do More with Less," *Scientific American* 305, no. 3 (2011): 52–53.

13. Nicos Komninos, Marc Pallot, and Hans Schaffers, "Special Issue on Smart Cities and the Future Internet in Europe," *Journal of the Knowledge Economy* 4, no. 2 (2013): 16.

14. Sharon E. Gillett et al., *Measuring the Economic Impact of Broadband Deployment*, Project No. 99-07-13829, National Technical Assistance, Training, Research, and Evaluation, 2006, accessed February 12, 2014, http://cfp.mit.edu; Darrell M. West, *The Next Wave: Using Digital Technology to Further Social and Political Innovation* (Washington, D.C.: Brookings Institution Press, 2011); Christine Zhen-Wei Qiang, "Broadband Infrastructure Investment in Stimulus Packages: Relevance for

Developing Countries," *Info: The Journal of Policy, Regulation and Strategy for Telecommunications, Information and Media* 12 (February 2010): 41–56; Jungyul Sohn, Tschangho John Kim, and Geoffrey J. D. Hewings, "Information Technology and Urban Spatial Structure: A Comparative Analysis of the Chicago and Seoul Regions," in *Globalization and Urban Development*, edited by Harry W. Richardson and Chang-Hee Christine Bae, 273–88 (Heidelberg: Berlin Springer, 2005).

15. Erik Brynjolfsson and Adam Saunders, *Wired for Innovation*, (Cambridge, Mass.: MIT Press, 2010); Robert Crandall, William Lehr, and Robert Litan, *The Effects of Broadband Deployment on Output and Employment: A Cross-sectional Analysis of U.S. Data*, Washington, D.C.: Brookings Institution, 2007, accessed February 12, 2014, www.brookings.edu.

16. Forman, Goldfarb, and Greenstein, *Technology Adoption In and Out of Major Urban Areas*; Forman, Goldfarb, and Greenstein, "Understanding the Inputs into Innovation."

17. Forman, Goldfarb, and Greenstein, *Technology Adoption In and Out of Major Urban Areas*; Forman, Goldfarb, and Greenstein, "Understanding the Inputs into Innovation."

18. Forman, Goldfarb, and Greenstein, *Technology Adoption In and Out of Major Urban Areas*; Forman, Goldfarb, and Greenstein, "Understanding the Inputs into Innovation."

19. Paul DiMaggio and Bart Bonikowski, "Make Money Surfing the Web? The Impact of Internet Use on the Earnings of US Workers," *American Sociological Review* 73, no. 2 (2008): 227–50.

20. Mossberger, Tolbert, and McNeil, *Digital Citizenship*.

21. Ines Mergel, "Social Media Adoption and Resulting Tactics in the U.S. Federal Government," *Government Information Quarterly* 30, no. 2 (2013): 123–30; Karen Mossberger, Yonghong Wu, and Jared Crawford, "Connecting Citizens and Local Governments? Social Media and Interactivity in Major U.S. Cities," *Government Information Quarterly*, 2014, accessed February 12, 2014, www.sciencedirect.com; Mary Feeney, Eric Welch, and Megan Haller, *UIC Investigating the Use of Technology for Civic Engagement by Local Governments*, University of Illinois at Chicago, Institute for Policy and Civic Engagement, 2011, accessed February 12, 2014, www.uic.edu/cuppa/ipce; John Carlo Bertot, Paul T. Jaeger, and Justin M. Grimes, "Promoting Transparency and Accountability through ICTs, Social Media, and Collaborative E-government," *Transforming Government: People, Process and Policy* 1, no. 6 (2012): 78–91.

22. Jeffrey M. Berry, Kent E. Portney, and Ken Thomson, *The Rebirth of Urban Democracy* (Washington, D.C.: Brookings Institution Press, 1993).

23. Caroline J. Tolbert and Karen Mossberger, "The Effects of E-Government on Trust and Confidence in Government," *Public Administration Review* 66 (March 2006): 354–69.

24. Benedict Jimenez, Karen Mossberger, and Yonghong Wu, "Municipal Government and the Interactive Web: Trends and Issues for Civic Engagement," in *E-

Governance and Civic Engagement: Factors and Determinants in E-Democracy, edited by Aroon Manoharan and Marc Holzer, 251–71 (Hershey, Pa.: IGI Global Press, 2012).

25. Tiago Camacho, Marcus Foth, and Andry Rakotonirainy, "Pervasive Technology and Public Transport: Opportunities Beyond Telematics," *Pervasive Computing (IEEE)* 12 (January 2013): 18–25.

26. David Wilkie, Jason Sewall, and Ming C. Lin, *Transforming GIS Data into Functional Road Models for Large-Scale Traffic Simulation*, 2011, accessed February 14, 2014, http://gamma.cs.unc.edu; see open-data portals for San Francisco and New York. For the former, see City and County of San Francisco, *San Francisco Data*, November 16, 2013, https://data.sfgov.org/. For the latter, see New York City, *NYC Open Data*, November 16, 2013, https://data.cityofnewyork.us/.

27. Steve Winkelman, Allison Bishins, and Chuck Kooshian, "Planning for Economic and Environmental Resilience," *Transportation Research Part A: Policy and Practice* 44 (August 2010): 575–86.

28. Kevin C. Desouza, "Designing and Planning for Smart(er) Cities," *Planning Practice* 10 (April 2012): 1–12.

29. Jessica Granderson, Mary Ann Piette, and Girish Ghatikar, "Building Energy Information Systems: User Case Studies," *Energy Efficiency* 1, no. 4 (2011): 17–30.

30. Desouza, "Designing and Planning."

31. See www.llga.org.

32. Brian Walker and David Salt, *Resilience Thinking: Sustaining Ecosystems and People in a Changing World* (Washington, D.C.: Island Press, 2006).

33. Donald Ludwig, Brian Walker, and Crawford S. Holling, "Sustainability, Stability, and Resilience," *Conservation Ecology* 1 (January 1997), accessed February 13, 2014, www.ecologyandsociety.org.

34. Ayda Eraydin and Tuna Taşan-Kok, *Resilience Thinking in Urban Planning* (Dordrecht, Netherlands: Springer, 2013).

35. Ibid.

36. Simon Huston and Clive Warren, "Knowledge City and Urban Economic Resilience," *Journal of Property Investment and Finance* 31 (January 2013): 78–88.

37. Ozge Yalciner Ercoskun, *Green and Ecological Technologies for Urban Planning: Creating Smart Cities* (Hershey, Pa.: Information Science Reference, 2012).

38. Eraydin and Taşan-Kok, *Resilience Thinking in Urban Planning*.

39. Deborah Wallace and Rodrick Wallace, "Urban Systems During Disasters: Factors for Resilience," *Ecology and Society* 13, no. 1 (2008): 18.

40. Hafedh Chourabi, Taewoo Nam, Shawn Walker, José Ramón Gil-Garcia, Sehl Mellouli, Karine Nahon, Theresa A. Pardo, and Hans Jochen Scholl, "Understanding Smart Cities: An Integrative Framework," paper read at 45th Hawaii International Conference on System Sciences (HICSS), Grand Wailea, Maui, Hawaii, January 4–7, 2012.

41. Leysia Palen, "Online Social Media in Crisis Events," *Educause Quarterly* 31, no. 3 (2008): 12.

42. Sophia B. Liu, Leysia Palen, Jeannette Sutton, Amanda L Hughes, and Sarah Vieweg, "In Search of the Bigger Picture: The Emergent Role of On-line Photo Sharing in Times of Disaster," paper read at Proceedings of the Information Systems for Crisis Response and Management Conference (ISCRAM), May 2008, at Washington, D.C., accessed October 15, 2014, www.cs.colorado.edu.

43. Mossberger, Tolbert, and McNeil, *Digital Citizenship*.

44. Eszter Hargittai, "Second-Level Digital Divide: Differences in People's Online Skills," *First Monday* 4, no. 7 (2002).

45. Paul DiMaggio, Eszter Hargittai, W. Russell Neuman, and John P. Robinson, "Social Implications of the Internet," *Annual Review of Sociology* (2001): 307–36.

46. FCC, *Connecting America*.

47. Karen Mossberger, Caroline J. Tolbert, and William Franko, *Digital Cities: The Internet and the Geography of Opportunity* (New York: Oxford University Press, 2013); Karen Mossberger, Caroline J. Tolbert, and Allison Hamilton, "Measuring Digital Citizenship: Mobile Access and Broadband," *International Journal of Communication* 6 (2012): 2492–528.

48. Maeve Duggan and Aaron Smith, *Cell Internet Use 2013*, Pew Research Center, 2013, accessed February 13, 2014, http://pewinternet.org.

49. Mossberger, Tolbert, and Franko, *Digital Cities*.

50. Tolbert and Mossberger, "Cuyahoga County Survey of Internet Access and Use."

51. Mossberger, Tolbert, and Franko, *Digital Cities*; Mossberger, Tolbert, and Hamilton, "Measuring Digital Citizenship."

52. Mossberger, Tolbert, and Franko, *Digital Cities*. Estimates for internet use (anywhere) and broadband adoption at home are produced for both central cities and their suburbs (MSA balance areas) for the 50 largest metropolitan areas, and by race and ethnicity. Multilevel statistical models include individual-level data from the Current Population Survey and aggregate-level variables to control for demographic and economic factors unique to each region. The central-city aggregate data was obtained from the American Community Survey (3-year estimates, 2007–9) and the *State and Metropolitan Area Data Book* suburban area model estimates. Aggregate-level variables in the statistical models include population size, per capita income, and the percent of the MSA or central city that is African American, Latino, educated with a high school diploma, over sixty-five years of age, and employed in the information sector. See Mossberger, Tolbert, and Franko, *Digital Cities*, 90, for more information.

53. Mossberger, Tolbert, and Franko, *Digital Cities*.

54. Larry C. Ledebur and William R. Barnes, *The New Regional Economies*, (London: Sage Publications, 1998); Manuel Pastor, Peter Dreier, J. Eugene Grigsby III, and Marta Lopez-Garza, *Regions That Work: How Cities and Suburbs Can Grow Together* (Minneapolis: University of Minnesota Press, 2000).

55. John. R. Logan and Brian J. Stults, *The Persistence of Segregation in the Metropolis: New Findings from the 2010 Census* (Brown University, 2011), accessed February 13, 2014, www.s4.brown.edu; Mossberger, Tolbert, and Franko, *Digital Cities*.

56. Elizabeth Kneebone, *The Great Recession and Poverty in Metropolitan America* (Washington, D.C.: Brookings Institution Press, 2010); Scott W. Allard and Benjamin Roth, *Strained Suburbs: The Social Service Challenges of Rising Suburban Poverty* (Washington, D.C.: Brookings Institution Metropolitan Policy Program, 2010).

57. Tolbert and Mossberger, "Cuyahoga County Survey of Internet Access and Use."

58. Tolbert, Mossberger, and Hamilton, unpublished estimates, 2013.

59. Federal Reserve and Brookings Institution, *The Enduring Challenge of Concentrated Poverty in America: Case Studies from Across the U.S.* (Washington, D.C.: Brookings Institution, 2008).

60. Janet Currie, H. Newburger, E. Birch, and S. Wachter, "Health and Residential Location," in *Neighborhood and Life Chances: How Place Matters in Modern America*, edited by H. B. Newburger, E. L. Birch, and S. M. Wachter, 3–17 (Philadelphia: University of Pennsylvania Press, 2011).

61. Brian A. Jacob and Jens Ludwig, "Educational Interventions: Their Effects on the Achievement of Poor Children," in Newburger, Birch, and Wachter, *Neighborhood and Life Chances*, 37–49; Paul A. Jargowsky, and Mohamed El Komi, "Before or After the Bell? School Context and Neighborhood Effects on Student Achievement," in Newburger, Birch, and Wachter, *Neighborhood and Life Chances*, 50–72.

62. William Julius Wilson, *The Truly Disadvantaged: The Inner City, the Underclass, and Public Policy* (Chicago: University of Chicago Press, 1987); Bayer Patrick, L. Ross Stephen, and Topa Giorgio, "Place of Work and Place of Residence: Informal Hiring Networks and Labor Market Outcomes," *Journal of Political Economy* 116, no. 6 (2008): 1150–96.

63. Robert J. Sampson, Stephen W. Raudenbush, and Felton Earls, "Neighborhoods and Violent Crime: A Multilevel Study of Collective Efficacy," *Science* 5328, no. 277 (1998): 918–24.

64. Yvette Alex-Assensoh, "Race, Concentrated Poverty, Social Isolation, and Political Behavior," *Urban Affairs Review* 3 (February 1997): 209–27.

65. Karen Mossberger, Caroline J. Tolbert, Daniel Bowen, and Benedict Jimenez, "Unraveling Different Barriers to Internet Use Urban Residents and Neighborhood Effects," *Urban Affairs Review* 48 (June 2012): 771–810.

66. Tolbert, Mossberger, and Anderson, *Measuring Change in Internet Use and Broadband Adoption*.

67. Mossberger, Tolbert, and Franko, *Digital Cities*.

68. Ibid.; Mossberger, Tolbert, Bowen, and Jimenez, "Unraveling Different Barriers to Internet Use Urban Residents and Neighborhood Effects."

69. Larry Ledebur and William Barnes, *The New Regional Economies: The U.S. Common Market and the Global Economy* (London: Sage, 1998).

70. The Smart Communities program was operated by the City of Chicago, in collaboration with the Chicago Local Initiative Support Corporation and neighborhood groups. The partnership also included the MacArthur Foundation and the Chicago Community Trust, and funding was provided by the Broadband Technol-

ogy Opportunities Program, administered by the National Telecommunications and Information Administration of the U.S. Department of Commerce, as part of the American Recovery and Reinvestment Act.

71. The study used a citywide survey and multilevel models over time, and controlled for a number of factors, including demographic differences between the neighborhoods (whether all low-income communities were catching up) and for demographic change (whether gentrification or other population change could account for the results). Some other activities online did not change at the neighborhood level—internet use for work, or political participation online among them.

72. Karen Mossberger, Mary K. Feeney, and Meng-Hao Li, *FamilyNet Evaluation Report*, 2014, accessed February 13, 2014, http://cpi.asu.edu; Karen Mossberger, Jennifer Benoit-Bryan, and Adrian Brown, *Smart Communities Evaluation: Civic 2.0 Participant Surveys and Interviews with Partner Organizations*, 2014, accessed February 13, 2014, http://cpi.asu.edu.

73. Katz and Bradley, *Metropolitan Revolution*.

74. See www.onecommunity.org.

75. Rebecca M. Hendrick, *Managing the Fiscal Metropolis: The Financial Policies, Practices, and Health of Suburban Municipalities* (Washington, D.C.: University of Georgetown Press, 2011).

76. Mossberger, Tolbert, and Franko, *Digital Cities*.

PART TWO

WHITE PAPERS

Connecting Technologies
to Citizenship

JANE E. FOUNTAIN

NATIONAL CENTER FOR DIGITAL GOVERNMENT,

UNIVERSITY OF MASSACHUSETTS AMHERST

INTRODUCTION

This white paper provides a broad overview of the theme "connecting technologies to citizenship" for readers who include academics, public intellectuals, policy officials, policy analysts, managers, and elected council members and mayors. In the paper, I report the results of a survey of recent work ranging across relevant, practical empirical studies, and promising practices. In the sections that follow, I draw inferences and conclusions from the collection of experiences and analysis available, although many trends and practices are just emerging, and highlight innovative or "tried-and-true" policies and practices that cities and metropolitan regions might consider going forward. Given the topic, one should say at the outset that while digital technologies and social media have enormous promise in many areas of social, economic, and political life, they may have little influence on some of the most intractable problems that cities face. In particular, unless people devote themselves to the task, these technologies may do little, for example, to change the "structures that reinforce poverty."[1] This paper focuses on technology but does not intend to portray it as a panacea.

Among the key topics addressed in this white paper are the following: First, what is the state of connection between citizen and governments? Second, how does technology change and influence core elements of city government from the nature of governance itself to the challenges of service delivery to prospects for political participation and deepening citizenship? Third, how are government services and information providers, brokers, and decision makers in city government taking advantage of appropriate technologies to better meet citizen needs and demands?

THE STATE OF THE CONNECTION BETWEEN
CITIZEN AND GOVERNMENT

In looking across the State of the City speeches delivered by mayors around the nation in 2013, one finds that these leaders emphasize the importance of strong and healthy communities relying on creativity, trust, and transparency to be achieved in part through building strong partnerships.[2] The theme of the 2013 annual conference of the International City and County Management Association built on the enduring legacy of "reinventing government"—during the group's twentieth anniversary year—and reemphasized the significance for cities of a clear and well-defined mission, an orientation toward results and outcomes and a focus on citizens.[3] Both national meetings cast their prescriptive advice in the context of continued economic constraints; immigration, aging, and other sources of fundamental demographic change; serious and growing disparities between the poor and the wealthy, and the dangers of indifference to that gap; and, not least, the potential and challenges of pervasive and powerful technologies.

Transparency has risen to the high-priority list of goals.[4] But transparency produces multiple effects. Transparency makes governments accountable. But it is also a precursor to engagement. While it cannot solve economic problems, opening the books and inviting individual and corporate citizens to understand more about flows of money and decision making in city budgets is necessary to meaningful collaboration, engagement, and partnerships. Moreover, calls for transparency provide an occasion for agency managers to work with their staffs to examine their data and results more analytically with a view toward evidence-based policy making and management. To this end, transparency efforts, including open data, in agencies have become a critical prerequisite for citizen participation, productive partnerships, and more analytical, data driven approaches to city management.

Advances in technology also produce crosscutting implications for cities. An astute observer of city management notes, "We now have the ability to contact nearly every household multiple times a day to encourage community engagement and help frame conversations around service delivery. At the same time, we no longer can control those conversations. Social media is accessible by people of both good and bad intent, and we ignore it at our peril. Meanwhile, the potential of 'big data' is enormous, enabling us to amass large amounts of information that will afford us greater transparency and accountability and give local officials an opportunity to partner with many different stakeholders."[5] A clear mission and a focused vision are at the core of public management. When resources are constrained, sustained focus on high-priority areas and discipline in maintaining that focus increase in importance. Added emphasis on performance management and measures can help when metrics measure strategic priorities and not simply items easily measured. Change takes time and sustained effort, so strong and stable leadership is key.

Although trust in government may be at all-time low levels, trust in local government is typically higher than it is for larger aggregates. This trust is part of the social glue that ensures commitment and mobilization of a city toward positive change and underlies technology-oriented innovations as importantly as innovation in other domains. A demanding economic environment forces city governments to put aside or discontinue programs and methods that are no longer relevant or working. New forms of budgeting, participation, and operations invite—and force—strong city governments to innovate, an essentially risky business of leaving old and comfortable routines and building new ones better suited to contemporary demands. These basics of public management are introduced here because they form the context in which technology projects are most likely to succeed and because information and communication technologies are part of most innovations in city government.

Technology cannot substitute for trust—or for strong city leadership and management—but it can help to build and sustain it by enabling transparency, communication, and coordination. In Salt Lake City, Utah, officials and experts examined the possibilities for using crowdfunding to attract start-up funds for emerging technology companies. Shared data and processes underlie implementation of multijurisdictional business licensing in Henderson, Nevada, and harmonization of city and county code services offices in Wichita, Kansas, enabling their consolidation. Durham, North Carolina, has developed a coordinated strategy to address and help "disconnected youth" by positioning them to become contributing members of the community by age twenty-five. Part of this effort relies on using technology to connect the key stakeholders in the ecosystem of organizations that assist youth. While public schools and nonprofits operate programs, the constellation of opportunities has been fragmented, presenting an opportunity for professional and technical networks to share mission and operations.[6]

THE PERSISTENCE OF THE DIGITAL AND DEMOCRATIC DIVIDE

The digital divide remains a challenge for many cities.[7] After twenty years of the Internet and web, it is clear that the digital divide will not self-correct. Recent focus on Internet navigation skills and those who actively use the web for political information gathering and communication versus those who do not provides troubling evidence of the persistence of the digital divide and its morphing into a more troubling "democratic divide."[8]

Karen Mossberger and her coresearchers wrote recently: "In an age when the United Nations has declared access to the Internet a human right, and universal access to high-speed broadband is a national goal urban areas have been largely ignored by federal [broadband or digital access] policy. Federal policies have focused on rural infrastructure. Yet, the U.S. is a metropolitan nation, and urban applications offer unparalleled advantages for addressing both innovation and inequalities in broadband access. This neglect may result in the failure to realize the social benefits of broadband and a broadly connected digital society."[9] The National Broadband Plan is a broad framework developed by the Federal Communications Commission (FCC) at the direction of Congress and through extensive public consultation. The plan did not include any funding for broadband initiatives. According to the FCC, the plan is meant "to ensure every American has 'access to broadband capability.' Congress also required that this plan include a detailed strategy for achieving affordability and maximizing use of broadband to advance 'consumer welfare, civic participation, public safety and homeland security, community development, health care delivery, energy independence and efficiency, education, employee training, private sector investment, entrepreneurial activity, job creation and economic growth, and other national purposes.'"[10]

Two programs federally funded at $7.2 billion under the American Recovery and Reinvestment Act of 2009 (ARRA, PL 111-5) were designed to fund a series of projects meant to build up the nation's broadband infrastructure and to improve broadband access: the Broadband Technology Opportunity Program (BTOP) and the Broadband Initiatives Program (BIC).[11] The programs focused on underserved communities to help them overcome distance and technology barriers by increasing connectivity.[12] The BTOP includes three programs—Sustainable Broadband Adoption (SBA), Public Computer Centers (PCC), Comprehensive Community Infrastructure (CCI). The SBA and PCC focused on stimulating demand, through increasing adoption and usage (particularly among vulnerable communities) and building access in public places, or "community anchor institutions."[13] The CCI built broadband infrastructure. Most of the projects developed using this ARRA funding were middle-mile projects, which by definition connect population centers to each other over rural areas. For example, in Illinois, the Illinois Century Network connects urban networks together, and connects rural-serving networks to urban centers by design to improve overall network performance by adding path diversity to Internet providers in Chicago, St. Louis, and Indianapolis. In this way, funding ostensibly directed toward rural projects assists urban areas, as well.[14]

Technological innovations and the benefits of social networks online do not reach those without access and digital literacy. In cities, often cost is a key challenge that keeps low-income individuals and minorities from adequate broadband access. Moreover, the quality of broadband access is often suboptimal in low-income urban neighborhoods.

Some researchers have claimed that national broadband policies and, specifically, the National Broadband Plan, have discounted the importance of cities. The argument is that market provision of broadband has priced many of the urban poor out of the market or provided suboptimal connection speeds. Most city governments cannot provide adequate access without federal support. They argue that rural broadband access is important, but many more citizens are left behind in underserved cities. Moreover, analysis of usage patterns by some researchers shows that rural provision of broadband tends to supply those with better education and income. Both within and across cities, barriers to access differ across low-income and minority communities suggesting the importance of community-based analysis and tools.

The high population density of cities is well aligned to produce economic and social benefits from broadband. In fact, lower-income earners might have the most to gain from robust broadband access but are more likely to suffer from inadequate access. For these reasons, some researchers argue that policies that are better aligned with the potential of cities would yield proportionately higher benefit for the country than those focused on rural areas.

Racial and ethnic disparities in access are glaring and persistent. Nationally, while only 65 percent of all Americans in 2010 had access adequate to produce digital citizenship, about half of U.S. minorities are either not at all or poorly connected to the Internet and digital resources and communication. Lower-income individuals face poor as well as unaffordable access. Moreover, individuals require exposure to training and programs to build digital literacy. Urban Latinos are the most disadvantaged technologically according to recent research. Broadband access is important, but digital literacy and familiarity are also needed for individuals to use the Internet to seek jobs, search for health information, gain access to education resources, and to participate politically online.

Many observers and policy makers point to the rise of smartphones and other mobile devices as the progenitors of Gov 2.0, in which social-media and user-generated content, produced primarily on mobile devices, eclipses the more traditional focus on information and communication technologies (ICT) and e-government. While many households include laptop and other computers as well as individuals using smartphones, data indicate that about 4 percent of the U.S. population uses cell phones as the primary means to access the Internet. These users tend to be African Americans and Latinos with low education and income levels. Recent analysis indicates that "mobile-only Internet users have dramatically lower levels of online activity and skill . . . [fostering] a second-class form of access, affecting many minorities and urban poor."[15] Contrary to claims of m-government or mobile access replacing broadband access from the home, these users tend to exhibit lower digital literacy and tend not to use the Internet in ways that might enhance their economic, educational, or political prospects.

Thus, while city governments should build channels for interaction through mobile phones, these are unlikely to reverse the digital divide and may exacerbate it. Digital citizenship means using e-government and related information and services to improve prospects for education, economic well-being, health, and political participation.[16] Individuals need home access to broadband to build such skill through sustained use and to support their full participation in social, economic, and political affairs.

The top fifty U.S. cities in terms of population vary enormously along several dimensions. City cores differ from their suburbs. Within cities, neighborhoods vary substantially. Research shows that even the most digitally innovative and advanced cities find provision of broadband for all a challenge. Researchers using spatial information have begun to map the geography of technological opportunity, connection, and use at the neighborhood level. They find that neighborhood-level characteristics—such as the availability of affordable, high-quality broadband access in a neighborhood—influence economic, social, and political representation, for example, the ability to use a city's website to access services and to interact and coordinate citizen participation, to access political information from local officials and other citizens, and similar online behavior. Mobilization at the neighborhood level requires connectivity. These findings demonstrate that individual-level differences in digital literacy should be viewed in the context of neighborhood-level attributes.

What should cities do about these persistent disparities? Karen Mossberger, Caroline Tolbert, and William Franko recommend that city officials across the country work together to change federal policies so that they reflect what cities need. Digital access and use should be analyzed at the level of the neighborhood in cities with programs for innovation, and improvement should focus on what works in particular types of neighborhoods. For example, research shows that the dimensions of use are different in low-income predominantly Latino neighborhoods versus primarily low-income African American neighborhoods. Programs that work must respond to actual patterns of use. Finally, it is clear that market provision of broadband access will not respond to geographic areas that are deemed uncompetitive. In these areas, other options will be needed to influence price and accessibility.

SERVICES FOR CITIZENS

An increasing number of cities offer "Web portals and online services, including the ability to pay utility bills, parking tickets, and taxes; to apply for building permits, license renewals, and jobs with the city; and to register property."[17] Key performance measures for provision of these types of services are convenience, cost of system operations and maintenance, and security. Cities are developing capacity to conduct such transactions over mobile phones and other devices. Provision through more channels introduces potentially new efficiencies and convenience for citizens, but cost of operations and security are a concern for city managers.

A review of recent research on the implementation of these technologies in cities across the country yields a useful starting point for comparing digital governance in 2013.[18] Research evaluating the municipal websites of Washington, D.C., and the two largest cities in each state compared cities using 104 measures of digital governance across five broad categories: content, services, usability, engagement, and privacy and security. Based on the results of this survey, the top ten cities for digital governance, averaging across the measurement categories, are Seattle, St. Paul, Milwaukee, Minneapolis, Washington, D.C., Portland (Oregon), St. Louis, Virginia Beach, Boston, and Fort Smith (Arkansas).[19] Digital governance scores for all of the cities surveyed increased from 2008 to 2010–11. Midwestern cities consistently outscored their counterparts in the West, South, and Northeast. Citizen and social engagement formed the weakest category for most cities.[20] The low score "can be attributed to the lack of support for interactive online citizen participation practices among municipalities." Although 80 percent of surveyed cities "provide one-way communication to the public via social media, it is unclear whether they allow citizens to communicate with elected officials using this feature."[21] Yet although citizen engagement is still weaker than other measures, it has seen the highest increase from 2008 to 2010–11.

Why do some municipal governments adopt IT policies to enable e-government and online services while others do not? What are the factors that explain variance in behavior and outcomes across municipal government?[22] Institutional developments that place IT expertise—either a chief information officer or a chief technology officer—within a mayor's executive group with participation in strategic developments are critical. An appropriate combination of centralization of some systems and standards with decentralization of agency and program level tools and capacity is important, as well. Researchers have observed that "managerial innovation orientation" in a range of policy areas is related to innovation in e-government.[23] The optimistic view of e-government adoption in cities entails the following narrative. Interactive government websites become standard operating procedure. Citizens expect digital services and interaction. E-government is transformative and able to markedly improve service delivery and public participation of citizens and business thereby increasing efficiency, effectiveness, transparency, and democratic processes related to participation and interaction.[24] The challenges that cities face in this narrative include the digital divide manifested in lack of access to broadband connections and lack of digital literacy; lack of budgetary resources to develop, maintain, and manage digital sites and services; and resistance by program managers and others to new practices and processes implied by use of new digital government applications and platforms.

SOCIAL MEDIA, CIVIC TECHNOLOGIES, AND OPEN DATA

Social media use has burgeoned since the advent of Facebook, Twitter, smartphones, and other platforms and tools that encourage social communication and user-generated content including visual information. Recent studies suggest that despite widespread implementation of social media networks on city websites it is unclear whether the early use of social media in cities has enhanced communication or governance.[25] According to the results of a survey measuring the percentage of city government websites using social media among the 75 most populous U.S. cities, between 2009 and 2011 use of Twitter increased from 25.3 to 86.7 percent, use of Facebook grew from 13.3 to 86.7 percent, and the proportion of city websites posting to YouTube jumped from 16 to 74.7 percent. The fact that there is little cost to cities to use these social media sites, and given that they can be easily placed on city government websites, it is not surprising to see such rapid uptake. However, despite this increase, the researchers note that "city websites have in the past provided little for two-way interactions" and question the efficacy of these new social networks to engender online participation in governance and contributions to policy formation.[26]

In spite of weak levels of deliberation and political participation on social media in city websites, many experts are optimistic about the potential of social media to deepen citizenship and democratic participation. The availability of web 2.0 platforms and applications, in particular, those using social media, have influenced greater use of tools with the potential to promote direct democracy and representation online.[27] Cities can "extend the public space [to build] consultation and dialogue between citizens and their governments."[28]

Some scholars suggest that the usefulness and effectiveness of employing web 2.0 platforms will rely on increasing transparency between citizen deliberation on such platforms and eventual policy outcomes.[29] In most governments the actual "decision making process for ultimately adopting a policy still remains opaque," and, according to some digital government experts, the success of implementing web 2.0 technologies for governance will rely on the extent to which citizens can expect their comments and online interactions to matter in policy outcomes.[30] Cultivating this level of expectation, which derives from citizens' beliefs in the legitimacy of the forum that they are participating in as well as their clear understanding of the criteria by which their input will be evaluated in the policy formation process, is key.

311: HOW CIVIC ARE "CIVIC TECHNOLOGIES"?

Social media and the potential to build applications using publicly available data have been the catalysts for an emerging industry of firms and nonprofits that develop, disseminate, and manage what are often called "civic technologies." It is important to be clear about what these systems actually do because the language used to describe them tends to obscure their actual functions. The language of Gov 2.0 and civic technologies is rife with hyperbole, utopian language, and promises of deeper democracy, engaged citizens, accountable governments, and empowerment for all at low cost. While this ecology of tools offer considerable power, city managers and officials need to thoroughly examine promises to estimate costs and expected outcomes. Moreover, they need to examine who will own and control public information and data, what the true costs of a revenue sharing contract entail, and how stable the support for a system is likely to be. A final decision for city managers is whether to use proprietary systems or open source systems. For these types of decisions, competent IT managers are critical.

Popular Open-Source Civic Technologies

Open source means that the source code, the software, is "open" or available for those with coding expertise to examine and modify. Open-source systems and applications often are developed by communities of developers, with the source code remaining open for improvement, troubleshooting, and refinements.

Open-source software is an alternative to proprietary software, often generating substantial savings for governments and greater flexibility in customizing and adapting software. The most visible example is the WhiteHouse .gov website, which was the first major open-source federal government site. Many other federal sites are open source. Some state and local governments have used open source for many years prior to the Obama administration's embrace of open source. Thus, a considerable base of knowledge and experience has accrued for open-source system use in government.

City governments that would like to use such tools to increase transparency, service responsiveness, and civic engagement have a variety of open-source tools and platforms available. The benefits of open source are low cost, easy adaptation, and avoidance of "lock in" to long-term contracts and upgrades.

Below are several brief examples of widely disseminated systems and recent apps that have received high visibility. Ten open-source tools recommended for cities follow.[31]

- CitySourced—a reporting tool to assist people in reporting civic issues, including public safety and environmental issues
- FixMyStreet—an open-source app that allows people to report issues related to road maintenance
- OpenPlans—typically used in larger cities, these planning and transportation tools can be adapted to smaller cities
- Electorate.Me—a website for people to exercise voice in political and social affairs
- NationBuilder—a group of open-source tools for communities including maps, surveys, and updates to facilitate interaction between agencies and individuals
- OpenPublic—an affordable content management system for cities to use in outreach to the public

- Open311—a reporting and tracking system for civic issues
- Granicus—provides cloud storage for media and a suite of tools to broadcast and manage media online
- SeeClickFix—a reporting tool that has been expanded to include workflow management, reporting, and other tools for nonemergency service management
- Open City—volunteers who develop apps at the request of cities

311 Digital Hubs

A 3-1-1 telephone number is one version of an N-1-1 special number (e.g., 9-1-1 for emergency calls) used in many U.S. communities to connect citizens to nonemergency government services through one central phone number typically directed to a call center or dispatcher. It was originally developed to decrease nonemergency calls to 911 emergency lines. The original 311 telephone-based systems, built before the Internet, were implemented independently across city governments as stand-alone efforts lacking interoperability.[32]

The Open311 platform uses open-source software to make innovations developed in one city using Open311 available to other cities. As one developer observed: "By adopting the Open311 API [application programming interface] for exposing civic data, cities are enabling civic developers like myself to build reusable tools and apps. To access data from 30 cities, [my app] doesn't need an adapter for each individual city, only a server URL that it can expect to interact and deliver data in the same way as described by the Open311 API documentation."[33] Indeed, since its launch in 2010 and influenced by IT officials in the Obama administration to build apps that can be used in any city, Open311 has been implemented in more than thirty cities globally and has catalyzed an array of apps and services.

Originally developed in Baltimore in 1996 and expanded as Citistat—a fully developed reporting, tracking, analysis, and management framework—contemporary Open311 digital hubs build on the concepts of a one-stop shop; responsiveness to citizens; and calls for transparency and performance management by recording, tracking, mapping, and using data to analyze demand and response patterns for city services using temporal and geo-spatial data. The primary efficiency gain in most implementations is the routing of all nonemergency calls to city departments and units through one number. Many, but not all, large U.S. cities have 311 capability. A recent article lists fifty U.S. cities using 311 systems.[34]

The City of Chicago launched its first 311 system in 1999. Chicago 311 has won several awards, including the Innovations in American Government award from the Kennedy School of Government in 2003. In fact, the 311 call center in Chicago backs up the 911 call center.

The New York City 311 site—NYC311—describes itself as the "main source of government information and non-emergency services . . . just a click, text, or call away." The New York City 311 hub maintains an active social media presence, with most elements of the hub on social media platforms such as Facebook and Twitter. The City of New York, following the Citistat model, uses information from 311 calls for performance measurement, tracking demand for services, response times, and other key metrics. New York was an originator of Compstat, a precursor to Citistat, in the New York City Police Department, an initiative that required police precincts to track, categorize, and map crime and to deploy police based on precinct-level data. Frequent review meetings with the chief of police and his staff were used to review data and precinct-level efforts to improve performance in response to their data. NYC311 extends the performance management tools to the range of nonemergency services managed by the city and extends the use of 311 to other categories including events, public health, and other information-based issues.

Kansas City's 311 hub similarly allows residents to interact with government via social media to help maintain city infrastructure and locate problems that would otherwise require significant outlays. Both hubs use Twitter, as well as other communication channels, to allow people to report problems and follow the status of their filing online. By using social media to crowdsource problems such as graffiti or potholes, these municipalities are able to address citizen concerns while both bettering infrastructure and saving money.[35]

Careful analysis of calls and complaints provides a vector for analyzing city services demand and response.[36] This analysis is useful under normal operating conditions as well as during emergencies. New York City received record high calls to its 311 number on the first day of a transit strike in 2005. In Orange County, Florida, the 311 system was in the pilot phase when three hurricanes struck Central Florida. The 311 number received more calls than any other, leading the county to implement the system fully.

The growth of Open311 raises questions about standardization of so-called civic technologies across state and local governments. While standardization across 311 and other platforms continues to increase across states, it is important to preserve diversity to keep state governments, "the laboratories of democracy," as Justice Brandeis called them, adapting to change according to their own lights.[37] Neither open nor proprietary 311 systems, on their own, reduce the digital divide or foster citizen participation and deliberation. But they offer low-cost, powerful communication routing, workflow management, and performance measurement through tracking and mapping.

Not surprisingly, by making enormous amounts of potentially valuable information available (e.g., calls to municipal governments and public databases) a small industry of firms and nonprofit organizations such as SeeClick-Fix Inc. and others has emerged quickly. The primary revenue source is advertising. A secondary and growing revenue source is assistance to cities in managing increasingly complex back-end analytical, reporting, and other management systems. So it may be that cities are enticed by the low cost of the initial Open311 offering and then find themselves virtually locked into a portfolio of management systems and tools that are not cost-free. Young firms in this space are developing civic technologies to delegate to and integrate across agencies and policy areas, across various communication channels (phone, text, email, etc.).

Distributional Biases and the Use of 311

Coproduction of city services is one of the promises of 311 and related services. While coproduction originally was tried in early efforts by public managers in the 1970s and 1980s, initiatives to outsource and privatize some city services took precedence over attention to coproduction.[38] Similarly, customer relationship management, or CRM, systems have given way terminologically to "civic technologies" or 311 systems, although the underlying frameworks and technological systems are highly similar. Citizens are considered coproducers in these models when they identify and report non-emergency municipal phenomena such as fallen trees, abandoned cars, trash that has not been picked up, and stray animals. Recent research finds little cause for concern that neighborhood-level inequalities, a reflection of deeper racial, ethnic, income, and inequalities, might be exacerbated by systems that heighten response to those who complain or report while possibly neglecting those who do not. The important exception, however, are Hispanics. A study of the Boston 311 system and its use from 2010 to 2011 found that race, education, and income disparities were not present in an analysis of 311 calls. But the researchers found that Hispanics "may use these systems less as requests move from call centers to the Internet and smartphones."[39] The study also found that low-income neighborhoods are less likely to use 311 services except for the case of smartphone use for reporting problems. Thus, the researchers conclude that smartphone use may help to bridge the digital divide, at least in the area of citizen coproduction for routine, well-structured, and easily measured city services. However, the use of a smartphone app to make 311 calls does not meet the criteria established for digital citizenship, a term that suggests a much higher level of digital literacy and interaction with economic, health, and government content.

Whether citizenship is deepened by such reporting, and if so, how it is influenced, remains to be analyzed. The term "transformation" is overused in this context, as in memes that suggest that cities have been transformed or that citizens have been transformed by reporting potholes and other problems and by tracking repair schedules and completion.

SeeClickFix Inc.

SeeClickFix is a firm that has developed for the market one of several toolkits that work in connection with 311 services. SeeClickFix is a private firm that offers a communications platform for reporting nonemergency problems, for governments to track and manage such reports, and to reply to citizens who post on the site. Citizens or groups report problems using mobile phones so the information is tagged by date, time, and geographic location. Those who report problems often send photos. SeeClickFix has developed mobile applications for reporting and a mobile platform that the firm will customize for a city to its specifications. They offer dashboards, mapping tools, report generation, and communication tools to offer dynamic "geo-based city notification tools" for municipal governments. Problems reported by citizens or others can be responded to with automated messages, routed to the appropriate departments, and used to create work orders and workflow management. The firm has partnered with several software firms, including Open311, Cityworks, and Microsoft Dynamics, to order and map workflows for municipal nonemergency problems.[40]

Originally, SeeClickFix sought to sustain itself with fees from advertising. In an August 2011 interview, the firm's founder, Ben Berkowitz, counted eight hundred local news sites as partners. The basic "widget" for SeeClickFix is free, with revenues for partners generated by selling ads. The firm also offers an ad-free widget to cities. In January 2011 the firm received $1.5 million from Omidyar Network and O'Reilly AlphaTech Ventures in equity funding. SeeClickFix quickly progressed to helping cities manage their 311 customer-response systems, an additional source of revenue that ranges from $1,200 to $20,000 per year depending on city size and complexity. In 2011 the firm had about sixty clients, including Philadelphia, Washington, D.C., New Haven, Hartford, Richmond, and Raleigh.[41] Albuquerque, New Mexico, launched the SeeClickFix platform and tools in April 2013. The firm claims that once the city has received six thousand reports of problems, the program, which costs $13,000, will have paid for itself. They note that Los Angeles recently paid $150,000 for a similar system.[42]

Berkowitz claims that simple civic engagement, for example, reporting a pothole that requires repair, may lead to deeper forms of engagement. His pithy phrase—"Potholes are the gateway drug to civic engagement"—encapsulates the view that people find their own uses for technological tools and may use them in surprising ways not envisioned by their developers. Having the ability to report a problem and to see it resolved may be empowering for citizens. Similarly, local networks of civically engaged individuals use SeeClickFix as a platform to coordinate their community efforts and to communicate with government in a public venue where requests and responses are tracked. Use of the platform and the communications it can facilitate have the potential to build trust not only from citizens to the government, but from the government back to the citizens during the course of many neighborhood projects.[43]

SeeClickFix is partnered with fifty-five municipalities in and around Boston. The day after the Boston Marathon bombings in April 2013, users of the site decided to post online if someone had a home available for people who needed a place to stay because of the bombing. Two hours later, 750 people had posted their homes in the Boston area as places for those to stay who had been dislocated by the bombing. During severe winter storms, people have coordinated online using SeeClickFix to help one another to shovel out. Berkowitz summarizes this phenomenon by relating ease of peer-to-peer communication to helpfulness: "Local connectivity increases neighborliness exponentially."

Code for America

Code for America presents another opportunity for city governments to gain technology capacity through civic technologies and voluntarism. It is the best known and probably the largest of a growing number of volunteer programs by which software developers donate time to help governments, typically by spending a year on a team working with a city government. Code for America is modeled after Teach for America, a nonprofit program that places college graduates in inner-city schools, typically for a year of teaching. Many web development experts would like to engage with governments to have impact. One of the founders of the organization, Jennifer Pahlka, noted: "In the vending machine model [of government services], if citizens want change (so to speak), all we can really do is shake the vending machine. If government architects a platform that allows participation, citizens can create the change they want to see."[44]

OPEN DATA

Civic technologies rely on public data to use transparency to increase accountability. To that end, many cities have begun removing barriers to transparency by generating open data, that is, open government databases, available for public use. Mossberger and Wu found open-data sites in only a dozen of the seventy-five largest cities by the summer of 2011, and noted that although "open data portals can promote transparency, their significance over time will depend on what data are made available, and the extent to which it is usable for intended audiences."[45]

Cities such as New York, Chicago, Seattle, and Boston have implemented open-data portals as part of their digital governance strategies. On the New York City government website, "over 750 datasets are available for free . . . from nearly 40 City agencies, including public safety data, buildings complaints, restaurant inspections and real-time traffic numbers."[46]

The cities of New York, Chicago, Seattle, and San Francisco have begun to compile their municipal data together on the website cities.data.gov. By sharing municipal data across the United States, the initiative increases government transparency and provides standardized data to the public and to developers who can then build applications that work across communities. Although it is not part of this shared open-data project, Boston has made data regarding its city reports, city information, and citizen requests for service available on its city government website. These data can be easily overlaid on a map of the city of Boston to provide citizens with a visual representation of data.

San Francisco

San Francisco has developed an expansive open-data portal, which allows a developer to use public data to create apps in order to enhance public services.[47] This open-data portal includes two hundred data sets.[48] The apps enhance communication, city services, and other important functions of governance. This portal has already engendered innovations including the development of the SFpark app, which provides commuters and drivers in the city with the latest information regarding available parking in the city as well as current rates for parking. It uses market and demand information to adjust parking prices once a month in order to ensure the most competitive prices are available in each area of the city. This allows commuters to plan their travel and to cut down on traffic at peak times of the day.

Development of web 2.0 technologies such as these suggests the usefulness and potential for widespread development of open-data portals at the municipal level. But it remains to be seen whether citizen- and business-generated apps will address some of the more intractable problems of cities and will help redress social and economic inequalities.

Citizens Connect: Boston

Additionally, moving beyond filling potholes, Boston has developed the Citizens Connect app, which allows users to report graffiti, potholes, and other blemishes that need correcting in the city. The website pronounces: "Citizens Connect is the City of Boston's award-winning effort to empower residents to be the City's 'eyes and ears.' Now you can alert the City of Boston to neighborhood issues such as potholes, damaged signs, and graffiti." In addition to allowing users to report these issues via tweet, text, or the app, it allows users to view other reports made by searching the map or by report type.[49]

Boston has implemented Citizens Connect on its website, a digital information and city services platform designed to initiate stronger citizen-to-government communication and help streamline citizens' access to city services and information. This platform was implemented by the Mayor's Office of Constituent Services and allows users to easily find online city resources; access city services and information; pay city utility bills, taxes, and fines, including parking tickets; and report issues with city services or problems in the city, like potholes or graffiti. It also allows citizens to request a variety of license renewals, search job postings, register animals, request city services like street cleanings, or access city information such as the city's Restaurant Health Ratings. All of these services and resources are incorporated on the city's homepage. The platform includes an online live chat component, called Citizens Connect Live, that provides 24-hour, 7-day contact online with staff in the Mayor's Office of Constituent Service to respond to queries about city services or to help with navigation to services and other resources online.[50]

Citizens Connect is also available to city residents as a mobile app. This app is mainly geared toward crowdsourcing rehabilitation efforts of city streets. It allows users to report damage such as potholes, graffiti, or damaged street signs by uploading a photo with a short description of the problem and its location. Residents may use Twitter to report problems by tweeting a picture and location while using designated tagging phrases such as "#sign." Once a report is generated, its status can be followed by users until city officials fix the problem. Citizens also have the ability to share the report with their peers via social media sites like Twitter. The Citizens Connect app allows for both citizen-to-citizen interaction and facilitates citizen-to-government interaction that many observers find lacking in web 2.0 implementations at the city level.

COMMONWEALTH CONNECT. In June 2013, the City of Boston and SeeClickFix announced the launch of the Commonwealth Connect App.[51] A success in Boston, it has been expanded into a statewide program called Commonwealth Connect, which allows fifty-four Massachusetts municipalities to use the platform and develop strategies to streamline citizen access to city or town services and resources while also allowing citizens to interact with the local government to report problems such as damage to city streets.

Boston has taken other steps to implement web 2.0 technologies in order to increase the effectiveness of city services. In addition to the Citizen Connect mobile app, which allows citizens to manually report issues such as potholes or graffiti, the city has also developed a mobile app called JustRide.

JUSTRIDE. In 2013, Boston was recognized by the National Association of State Chief Information Officers (NASCIO) for its efforts in mobile ticketing for the Mass Bay Transit Authority (MBTA) commuter rail and ferry services. A physical extension of metropolitan Boston's CharlieCard ticket-selling infrastructure would have cost $70 million. By taking advantage of mobile phones, however, the MBTA was able to deliver the same service with virtually no initial development costs by using a revenue sharing model in which the vendor receives 2.8 percent of sales revenues from mTicketing. This is the same revenue sharing model the MBTA uses with its neighborhood vendors.[52] The MBTA partnered with Masabi, an award-winning British company that specializes in mobile ticketing (mTicketing) for transportation systems, to produce the JustRide app. This app allows users to purchase tickets on their mobile devices that are easily recognizable by on-board staff. This project saves taxpayers money while providing solutions that work seamlessly with current uses of social technology.[53]

STREETBUMP. The City of Boston Mayor's Office of New Urban Mechanics has implemented an app that automatically senses bumps identified and located through a cell phone's accelerometer and its GPS system. This app does not require an individual to record and report a problem; the app senses the bump and communicates it to the Open311 system. The Mayor's Office of New Urban Mechanics partnered with the firms Connected Bits, IDEO, and InnoCentive, and Professor Fabio Carrera of the Worcester Polytechnic Institute. The mayor's office has promised to make the app available to other cities. It is interoperable on the Open311 system.

New urban mechanics is an innovation lab focused on urban innovations to help cities primarily through the use of civic technologies, collaboration with constituents, and neighborhood programs. The Boston Office of Urban Mechanics became part of the mayor's office in 2010, and since then the mayor's office in Philadelphia added such a department.

DELIBERATION: THE VIRTUAL TOWN HALL

Cities have implemented online forums since the early 1990s to engage citizens in deliberative discussions regarding public policies and issues affecting whole communities. These efforts began with online bulletin boards and listservs and have modernized as technologies have advanced. Yet only six cities among the seventy-five largest U.S. cities in Mossberger and Wu's 2011 study have incorporated a virtual town hall platform into the city website in order to facilitate civic participation online. While citizens may find many other ways to engage in deliberation—for example, through social media in neighborhood, community, or interest-based deliberations—some view the virtual town hall, a citywide site for deliberation (and not simply for reporting complaints and problems) to be one of the more important potential developments of digital governance. Although many researchers encourage city managers to develop such deliberation, relatively little is known about how best to manage such interactions, who participates and with what results.

Virginia Beach has implemented a virtual town hall portal that allows users to interact online with each other as well as with government officials to deliberate on public policies.[54] Anyone can view information and comments on the site but only citizens who register with their names and addresses can provide commentary, input, and other suggestions for different laws and issues discussed in the online forum. The site was developed and is managed by Peak Democracy, a firm that developed the Open Town Hall website. A person's name and neighborhood is included with his or her comments. This information is used to moderate and maintain control of interactions and posts. For example, identifying information makes it clear when comments are made by those who do not live in Virginia Beach. Peak Democracy has developed analytical and reporting tools to track geography and demography of those using the site. The firm reports that it has worked with more than one hundred government agencies. They report that local governments have implemented 1,718 open town hall forums to date and list client cities including Norfolk, Virginia; Salt Lake City; Santa Clara, California; Delray Beach, Florida; Decatur, Georgia; Tempe, Arizona; Aspen, Colorado; Saint Paul, Minnesota; Tulsa, Oklahoma; Ann Arbor, Michigan; and Tyler, Texas.[55]

EMERGENCY MANAGEMENT AND POLICING

The use of digital platforms by city police forces and local emergency management agencies has grown enormously in response to September 11, 2001, recent natural disasters, and the revolution in social media and big data. According to a study conducted by the Congressional Research Service, the use of web 2.0 technologies to enhance emergency response is currently implemented similarly to other web 2.0 technologies in cities: primarily as one-way passive information dissemination vehicles but with the ability to receive messages, wall posts, and responses to polls from citizens. This is the modal use by city governments as well as by the Federal Emergency Management Agency. However, the potential of social media use in disaster and emergency management includes "using the medium to conduct emergency communications and issue warnings; using social media to receive victim requests for assistance; monitoring user activities and postings to establish situational awareness; and using uploaded images to create damage estimates, among others."[56] Indeed, many developing countries already use such systems, originally developed by Ushahidi, a nonprofit organization in Kenya.[57]

Next Door

In the wake of recent disasters including Hurricane Sandy, New York and other cities have begun to implement social media platforms such as Next Door, a private, neighborhood-based social platform, that facilitates communication and exchange among neighbors. The small firm, Next Door, has attracted $60 million in venture capital, a sign of investor confidence in its potential. Cities have found neighborhood-level social networks valuable during natural and other crises to facilitate government responses. Users sign up with their real name and address to access online forums specifically for their neighborhoods. This local focus allows community members to acquaint themselves with one another and foster relationships and networks that can be activated in times of disaster or emergency.[58]

Seattle: Tweets by Beat

The Seattle Police Department has established a social media presence that incorporates the use of Twitter as a type of digitized police scanner with tweets sent to alert citizens of police-dispatch calls and reports of crimes in their neighborhood in real time. This program, named Tweets by Beat, allows users to observe police dispatch calls in their neighborhood and stay informed in cases of emergency. According to the Tweets by Beat website, "The Seattle Police Department is making it easier than ever before for you to find out about crime happening in your neighborhood. With Tweets by Beat, you can follow or view a Twitter feed of police dispatches in each of Seattle's 51 police beats, and find out about the flashing lights and sirens on your block."[59]

Seattle, Palo Alto, Houston, and Kansas City, Missouri, are examples of cities whose police departments have implemented social media into their communication strategies.[60]

THE ENABLING CITY: MAKING COPRODUCTION WORK

Nancy Roberts defines coproduction as a type of civic engagement: "Citizens and administrators cooperate with each other through neighborhood associations, community organizations, and other client groups to redesign and deliver government services. Their mutual goal is to improve the quality and quantity of service outputs. Citizen-agency collaborations in the production of services occur at all levels of government, but the most prevalent are at the local level. Coproduction has emerged as an attractive option during budget cutbacks, mounting service demands, and stretched resources. Its virtue also lies in the creation of network ties that are essential for building strong communities and maintaining a healthy democratic system."[61] Roberts brings together several strands of importance to cities grappling with new technological possibilities. When coproduction works, it uses the efficiencies and power of digital and social media platforms in the service of strengthening local and neighborhood communities.

Other experts on coproduction have emphasized the importance of understanding citizens and their lives "deeply." This "professional empathy" cannot be crowdsourced or gained from big data. But it is essential in order to design services and solutions. It requires close interaction between city staff and neighborhood residents. Rather than hailing a technocratic approach by which technologies dominate, a more human approach—and, many would argue, a more effective approach—extends coproduction to the very design of services and policies. In design models that work, rapid prototyping and iteration to improvement replace more traditional bureaucratic ideas that separate stakeholders, fragment problems, and locate expertise only with professionals. These developments in coproduction are important because Open311 and similar models can function merely as complaint handling and workflow processing systems rather than as community development vehicles.[62] While the efficiency of 311 systems constitutes part of their value, the close human contact necessary to understand specific neighborhoods and their challenges, while inefficient because it is labor-intensive, is vital to progress.

RECOMMENDATIONS

1. Attend to the digital divide. Access to apps and 311 systems, while important, are unlikely to be sufficient to ensure digital citizenship. Examine neighborhood-level connectivity and develop neighborhood-level programs to ensure access and digital literacy.

2. Determine how much interactivity you have between your city and your citizens. Then determine how much inactivity you want. Social media alone does not build deliberation and civic engagement although it offers effective platforms for starting such efforts. Government leaders must work with community groups to structure and promote deliberation. Participatory strategic planning is widely used. Participatory budgeting is gaining traction.

3. Assess civic technologies. While this ecology of tools offers considerable power and potential cost savings, city managers and officials should thoroughly examine estimated costs and expected outcomes. Vibrant and active communities of urban innovation labs, urban mechanics, civic technologies, and similar groups should be part of the network of a city's IT and social-media staff. Benchmark against other cities and learn from useful practices. Ask who will own and control public information and data, what the true costs of a revenue sharing contract entail, and how stable the support for a system is likely to be. A major decision for city managers is whether to use proprietary or open-source systems. For these types of decisions, competent IT and social media managers are critical.

4. Take advantage of open-source platforms and tools. Benchmark against cities of comparable scale to find cases and sources of information.

5. Encourage the development of apps to address city service provision, and seek out apps developed for other cities that may be used in your own

city. Increasingly, these apps are gathered into dictionaries and available for wide sharing.

6. Disengage from first-generation, expensive, proprietary workflow management systems when it is possible to do so. This can generate substantial cost savings and simplify and streamline government services for citizens.

7. Generate feedback and dialogue among citizens. Most deliberation sites are moderated to control against capture by narrow interest groups. The best results seem to be achieved by specifying specific problems or policy areas to structure and focus discussion and by setting a timetable for the discussion and the expected results (ideas, a plan, a decision, opinions, etc.). Generating alternatives or discussion of the pros and cons of various alternatives can be highly useful for public managers.

8. Keep in mind that technology is a tool, not an end goal. Citizen coproduction of services holds promise to increase trust and increased citizen engagement when governments have and use capacity to respond to requests for assistance. Technology alone will not build engagement or trust, but web-based platforms and tools can be useful catalysts and do provide powerful coordination assistance. Effective coproduction requires face-to-face interaction at the neighborhood level to closely engage with what citizens need in their specific context.

9. Identify and exploit opportunities to increase transparency in government. Transparency is powerful. Citizens will continue to demand open data and more transparent processes in government.

10. Develop and implement strategies and structures to ensure broad representation of perspectives and views in online forums. Open platforms for citizen engagement risk capture and distortion from narrow interest groups with intense beliefs who use social media forcefully and strategically.

Notes

The author is grateful to University of Massachusetts Amherst undergraduates Elysia Eastty and Andrew Clinton for helpful research assistance and to Professor Jon Gant for helpful discussion concerning federal broadband policies.

1. This phrase is borrowed from Paul Farmer and Fr. Gustavo Gutiérrez, *In the Company of the Poor* (Maryknoll, N.Y.: Orbis Books, 2013).

2. Raksha Vasudevan, "Building for the Future in an Uncertain Present: State of the Cities 2013," CitiesSpeak.org, official blog of the National League of Cities, March 21, 2013, accessed February 14, 2014.

3. Robert J. O'Neill Jr., "Local Governments' Enduring Reinvention Imperative," *Governing*, October 30, 2013, accessed February 14, 2014, www.governing.com.

4. See, for example, Jon Gant and Nicol Turner-Lee, *Government Transparency: Six Strategies for More Open and Participatory Government*, the Aspen Institute Communications and Society Program, February 2011, accessed February 15, 2014, www.aspeninstitute.org. See also Knight Commission on the Information Needs of Communities in a Democracy, *Informing Communities: Sustaining Democracy in the Digital Age*, Aspen Institute, 2009.

5. O'Neill Jr., "Local Government in an Era of Creative Destruction."

6. See Peter Coy, "The Kids Are *Not* Alright," *Bloomberg Businessweek*, February 7–13, 2011; "Disconnected Youth in the Triangle: An Ominous Problem Hidden in Plain Sight," a report to the North Carolina GlaxoSmithKline Foundation by MDC Inc., August 2008, accessed February 14, 2014, www.mdcinc.org; IBM Smarter Cities Challenge Durham report, no date, accessed February 14, 2014, http://durhamnc.gov.

7. This section on the digital divide in cities summarizes key findings of Karen Mossberger, Caroline Tolbert, and William W. Franko, *Digital Cities* (New York: Oxford University Press, 2013).

8. Seong-Jae Min, "From the Digital Divide to the Democratic Divide: Internet Skills, Political Interest, and the Second-Level Digital Divide in Political Internet Use," *Journal of Information Technology and Politics* 7, no. 1 (2010).

9. Mossberger, Tolbert, and Franko, *Digital Cities*.

10. FCC, National Broadband Plan, Executive Summary, accessed February 14, 2014, www.broadband.gov.

11. For information concerning BTOP at the U.S. Department of Commerce National Telecommunications and Information Administration, see www2.ntia.doc .gov/. For information regarding BIP at the U.S. Department of Agriculture Rural Development Service see www.rurdev.usda.gov/utp_bip.html.

12. Office of the Vice President, "Vice President Biden Kicks Off $7.2 Billion Recovery Act Broadband Program," December 17, 2009, accessed February 10, 2014, www.whitehouse.gov.

13. See BroadbandUSA: Connecting America's Communities, accessed January 9, 2014, www2.ntia.doc.gov/about.

14. The author is grateful to Professor Jon Gant for helpful comments concerning federal broadband initiatives.

15. Zachary Spicer, review of Mossberger, Tolbert, and Franko, *Digital Cities*, British Politics and Policy blog at LSE, accessed February 14, 2014, http://blogs.lse.ac.uk.

16. Karen Mossberger, Caroline J. Tolbert, and Ramona S. McNeal, *Digital Citizenship: The Internet, Society and Participation* (Cambridge, Mass.: MIT Press, 2008).

17. Tony E. Wohlers and Lynne Bernier, "Innovative City Hall: A Comparative Study of Policy Adoption in the U.S. and France," *Journal of Information Technology and Politics* 9, no. 4 (2012).

18. Marc Holzer, Marc Fudge, Robert Shick, Genie Stowers, and Aroon Manoharan, 2012, *U.S. Municipalities E-Governance Survey (2010–11): An Assessment and Ranking*

of Municipal Websites, accessed February 14, 2014, http://spaa.newark.rutgers.edu; Karen Mossberger, and Yonghong Wu, "Civic Engagement and Local E-Government: Social Networking Comes of Age," Institute for Policy and Civic Engagement, University of Illinois Chicago, working paper, February 2012, accessed February 14, 2014, www.uic.edu/cuppa.

19. Holzer et al., *U.S. Municipalities E-Governance Survey*.

20. In this category, the average score was only 4.69 out of a possible total score of 20, which is approximately only half as high as the average score of the lowest of the other categories (ibid., 79).

21. Holzer et al., *U.S. Municipalities E-Governance Survey*, 77–78.

22. Wohlers and Bernier, "Innovative City Hall."

23. Donald F. Norris and M. Jae Moon, "Advancing E-Government at the Grassroots: Tortoise or Hare?," *Public Administration Review* 65 no. 1 (2005).

24. See Wohlers and Bernier, "Innovative City Hall," for a review of drivers and barriers to ICT adoption in municipal governments in large- and medium-sized cities.

25. In "Civic Engagement and Local E-Government," Mossberger and Wu found that social media use in city government websites increased between two and five times from 2009 to 2011 in their analysis of the 75 largest cities in the United States.

26. Mossberger, and Wu, "Civic Engagement," figures on 6, quotation on 15.

27. M. Hilbert, "The Maturing Concept of e-Democracy: From e-Voting and Online Consultations to Democratic Value Out of Jumbled Online Chatter," *Journal of Information Technology & Politics* 6 (2009); J. K. Scott, "'E' the People: Do U.S. Municipal Government Web Sites Support Public Involvement?," Public Administration Review, 66 (2006).

28. D. G. Lenihan, "Realigning Governance: From e-Government to e-Democracy," in M. Khosrow-Pour, ed., *Practicing e-Government: A Global Perspective* (Hershey, Pa.: IDEA Group Publishing, 2005), 274.

29. L. Luna-Reyes, S. A. Chun, and J. Cho, "E-participation and Transparent Policy Decision Making," *Information Polity* 17, no. 2 (2012): 129–45.

30. Ibid., 139.

31. Logan Harper, "10 Tools to Help Open Source Cities Maintain Transparency," Opensource.com blog post, October 28, 2013, accessed February 14, 2014.

32. For a summary of the history of 311 and its evolution to Open311, including interview results with some of the developers, see Manik V. Suri, "From Crowdsourcing Potholes to Community Policing: Applying Interoperability Theory to Analyze the Expansion of 'Open311,'" Berkman Center for Internet and Society, Harvard University, Research Publication No. 2013-18, accessed February 14, 2014, http://cyber.law.harvard.edu.

33. Ben Sheldon, "Hard Data on the Status of Open311," Code for America, July 27, 2012, accessed February 14, 2014, http://codeforamerica.org.

34. "3-1-1," Wikipedia, accessed February 14, 2014, http://en.wikipedia.org.

35. The city of New York lists its official apps on the NYC Digital webpage and includes the NYC311 app as well as the NYPD app, NYC City Hall and NYC Stuff Exchange. The apps are available at www.nyc.gov.

36. Steven Johnson, "What a Hundred Million Calls to 311 Reveal About New York," Wired.com, November 1, 2010, accessed February 14, 2014.

37. *New State Ice Co. v. Liebmann*, 285 U.S. 262 (1932), at 311. Justice Brandeis observed: "To stay experimentation in things social and economic is a grave responsibility. Denial of the right to experiment may be fraught with serious consequences to the nation. It is one of the happy incidents of the federal system that a single courageous state may, if its citizens choose, serve as a laboratory; and try novel social and economic experiments without risk to the rest of the country."

38. John Alford, "A Public Management Road Less Traveled: Clients as Co-Producers of Public Services," *Australian Journal of Public Administration* 57, no. 4 (1998): 128–37. Cited in Benjamin Y. Clark, Jeffrey Brudney, and Sung-Gheel Jang, "Coproduction of Government Services and the New Information Technology: Investigating the Distributional Biases," *Public Administration Review* 75, no. 5 (2013): 687.

39. Clark, Brudney, and Jang, "Coproduction of Government Services and the New Information Technology."

40. A description of the management tools developed by SeeClickFix is available at http://seeclickfix.com/government/management-tools.

41. Tom Grubisich, "How SeeClickFix Built Revenue Streams from Potholes," *Street Fight*, August 11, 2011, accessed February 14, 2014, http://streetfightmag.com.

42. "Albuquerque, NM Launches App to Cut Costs, Engage Residents," SeeClickFix blog post, April 4, 2013, accessed October 21, 2014, http://blog.seeclickfix.com/blog.

43. All quotations in this paragraph are from Ben Berkowitz, TED Talk at the University of Connecticut, October 21, 2013, available on YouTube.

44. Jennifer Pahlka, "Give Us Your Hands, Not Just Your Voices," Code for America blog post, September 8, 2009, accessed October 22, 2014, www.codeforamerica.org.

45. Mossberger and Wu, "Civic Engagement," 4.

46. Technology & Public Service Innovation: Open Data, www.nyc.gov.

47. DataSF (the open-data portal for the city and county of San Francisco), accessed October 22, 2014, https://data.sfgov.org/.

48. Ibid.

49. Citizens Connect, accessed October 22, 2014, www.cityofboston.gov.

50. Ibid.

51. "Patrick Administration and City of Boston Announce 54 Municipalities Participating in Commonwealth Connect App," City of Boston press release, June 18, 2013, accessed February 14, 2014, http://blog.seeclickfix.com.

52. The revenue-sharing model is detailed in NASCIO, 2013 State IT Recognition Awards, Digital Government, "Project: mTicketing for Commuter Rail and Ferry Services," accessed October 22, 2014, www.nascio.org.

53. The announcement of NASCIO's award for Massachusetts mTicketing is noted in "Project: mTicketing for Commuter Rail and Ferry Services" press release, accessed October 22, 2014, www.nascio.org/awards/2013awards/.

54. City of Virginia Beach, Virginia, Virtual Town Hall, accessed October 22, 2014, www.vbgov.com.

55. Open Town Hall, accessed October 22, 2014, www.peakdemocracy.com.

56. Bruce R. Lindsay, "Social Media and Disasters: Current Uses, Future Options, and Policy Considerations," Congressional Research Service, September 6, 2011, accessed February 14, 2014, www.fas.org.

57. Ushahidi, accessed October 22, 2014, http://ushahidi.com.

58. See, for example, "Won't You Be in My Nextdoor Network?," Wall Street Journal, April 30, 2013, accessed February 13, 2014, http://online.wsj.com; Drake Baer, "As Sandy Became #Sandy, Emergency Services Got Social," Fast Company, November 9, 2012, accessed February 14, 2014, www.fastcompany.com.

59. The Seattle Police Tweets by Beat program is described at www.seattle.gov/police/, accessed February 11, 2014.

60. Robin Whithall, "Police Using Social Media: 4 Innovative Departments," ArchiveSocial blog, May 20, 2013, accessed February 14, 2014, http://archivesocial.com.

61. Nancy Roberts, "Public Deliberation in an Age of Direct Citizen Participation," *American Review of Public Administration* 34, no. 4 (December 2004): 315–53, quote on 330.

62. See Christian Bason, *Leading Public Sector Innovation: Co-creating for a Better Society* (Bristol, U.K.: Policy Press, 2010). See also MINDLab, Copenhagen, Denmark, accessed February 14, 2014, www.mind-lab.dk/en.

Toward a Market Approach
for Civic Innovation

DISCUSSANT: DANIEL X. O'NEIL

Jane Fountain wrote a paper for the 2013 UIC Urban Forum "Technology and the Resilience of Metropolitan Regions" panel titled "Connecting Technologies to Citizenship." In it, she describes many trends and practices that are emerging around the practice of civic innovation.

She writes of the persistence of the digital divide and the threat of a widening democratic divide, where residents do not receive the benefits of representation in communities where technology is absent. She also writes of the opportunities present in high population density, the rise of smartphones and other mobile devices, and the potential of "big data" to inform government services.

What I'd like to focus on in this response, however, is her question, "how civic are 'civic technologies'?" In my world, I frame that question in terms of popularity with regular residents. "Civic" means public—that it has broad utility, broad acceptance, and is widely recognized as being a part of the fabric of civic life. This is the frame that we should bring to technology that seeks to serve residents in dense cities.

In my work at the Smart Chicago Collaborative, I helped create the Open311 system for Chicago's municipal government. This led to the publication of millions of rows of public data and simple methods for developers and nascent companies to read and write directly to the enterprise service request system at the city—the technology backbone for the delivery of services in the third largest city in the United States. This is the largest implementation of Open311 anywhere.

The existence of Open311 in Chicago, however, has not led to the creation of many new tools. Only a handful of services connect to this system, and none have any traction with regular residents. Even though it was widely requested by the developer community and touted as a major opportunity for economic growth, there are no widely used resident-focused websites or systems that use Open311.

THE CURRENT STATE OF THE MARKET

The question is why, and I believe the answer is that there is no cohesive market for the civic-innovation sector of the technology industry. In fact, very few actors in the market even understand themselves to be a part of the technology industry. A dominant frame of the civic-hacker movement is the quick creation of tools, dashed off in hackathons or during feverish nights. The idea of being part of the trillion-dollar industry is anathema to this frame.

The natural end result of these efforts are interesting tools with good intentions that are of limited use to the masses in cities. The current status of the civic-innovation sector of the technology industry can be analyzed as follows:

- There is good movement in the provision of data (raw materials).
- There is an abundance of energy around the making of things (labor).
- There is a paucity of thought around why we make things or what

is the best thing to make (market research, user testing, continuous improvement).

- There is even less thought around the relationship between the things we make and the universe of other things within which it fits (market analysis).
- Lastly, all of our things exist in an environment where their popularity is puny next to the opportunity (market penetration).

This state of affairs was evident in Professor Fountain's paper, which reviewed a wide range of existing projects, tools, and companies. Included were municipal-driven projects like Citizens Connect, Commonwealth Connect, and the work in San Francisco as well as by companies such as SeeClickFix, CitySourced, and Granicus. She covered nonprofit projects like FixMyStreet and Electorate.Me.

This was a great scan that covered the field well, but it is illustrative of the jumble that defines the current state of the civic-innovation sector of the technology industry—it completely lacks a frame for understanding. And without a frame, it is difficult for the sector to grow and become sustainable.

FRAMING THE OPPORTUNITY

When we view this milieu—this robust and creative mix of people doing work to improve lives in cities through technology—a natural frame emerges.

First off, civic innovation is a sector of the technology industry. This expansive language embraces a neighborhood blogger who measures cars with a homemade traffic counter as well as people who work at large startups looking to change municipal laws to support their business models.

There is a job titled "senior counsel of product" at Airbnb—the community marketplace for people to list, discover, and book unique accommodations around the world—whose job it is "advise our product and engineering teams to manage legal risk and ensure regulatory compliance on a broad range of legal issues." That is a job generated by the civic-innovation industry—it is explicitly designed to interact with the municipal structure. Yet my guess is that no one at Airbnb feels they are a part of the civic-innovation sector—they just think they are part of a startup.

However, all of the graphic designers at Airbnb see themselves as part of a broader set of design professionals linked across companies, industries, and organizations. This frame is well-established in universities and other formal career development venues. Engineers segregate themselves into language-specific conferences like Pycon in order to deep-dive into their specialties. Civic-innovation practitioners meet at hackathons and hack nights, but their civic-innovation work is most often on the side, something other than what they do in their professional lives.

SUPPORT FOR STANDARDS

Just as in any other economic sector, the civic-innovation sector requires certain macro conditions under which it can thrive. These conditions are often wrought through formal regulatory and lobbying activities as well as the creation of standards. In this case, that revolves around data fluidity, format standards, ethical conduct, propagation of open-source software, and adherence to principles of open government.

Open311 is one such standard—it refers to a "standardized protocol for location-based collaborative issue-tracking." As Open311 is adopted in more cities, companies that work in this space could scale up faster.

More standards are needed. Yelp supports the Local Inspector Value-Entry Specification (LIVES), but it has had very little uptake by cities. Currently, only a few cities are complying with the standard, which allows restaurant inspection data to be included on Yelp. Adjusting specific and custom municipal processes to a generic data standard is hard work and requires staff, whereas such positions often don't exist in city government.

There are a number of accepted modes of operation that help the sector grow. Github, a web-based hosting service for software development projects, is the dominant method of collaborating on code. There's a whole set of values inherent in Github—sharing, openness, and humility—that inform the sector. There's an opportunity to build on these values to create real businesses.

There set of rapidly maturing institutions and organizations that support the creation of standards and sharing of work, including Smart Chicago, Code for America, and the Sunlight Foundation. All of this is the infrastructure for an industry we want to see.

DEEPER PARTNERSHIPS, MERGER AND ACQUISITION, AND CORPORATE GROWTH

The Homebrew Computer Club was an early computer hobbyist group in Silicon Valley that started in the mid-1970s. Members of this group went on to launch the personal-computer revolution, but not without a lot of ambition, capital, and planning.

There is often a disconnect between the skills inside the nascent civic-hacker movement and the needs of the market for civic technology. Often developers "solve" problems that didn't exist just because there was a dataset available to address the issue. There's very little attention to the needs of regular residents during the brainstorming phase. Developers scratch their own itch and never ask what's itching their neighbor.

Another issue is the skills gap. Older software companies—usually using older technologies—dominate the market for municipal software. Cities are naturally wary of making wholesale changes to existing systems that (ugly as they may be) actually work. Enterprising startups should seek to engage existing vendors to gradually improve their offerings through better design, added features, more fluid data-sharing—all of the values of sector.

An example is the municipal legislation management sub sector of the civic-innovation sector of the technology industry. It is dominated by Granicus, a vendor referenced in Professor Fountain's paper. The main purpose of their product is to help their municipal legislator customers manage complex legislative processes, and they seem to serve that purpose well.

The public-facing websites generated by the Granicus system are less successful, by modern Web standards. This has led to the opportunity for an open-source system, Councilmatic, developed by Code for America fellows, and published for free on Github. Councilmatic could not exist without the legislative data published by a Granicus system—it absolutely relies on it. There's no reason why Granicus shouldn't "acquire" the talent behind Councilmatic and embed it into their product, making it better. But that hasn't happened yet.

As the civic-innovation sector of the technology industry matures, these types of pairings will become natural, and provide benefits to people in cities all over the world. It's time for the period of great creativity and bursts of brilliance to meld into a period of focused value and sustained growth for the civic innovation sector of the technology industry.

A Factory in Every Home?

Emerging Manufacturing Technologies and Metropolitan Development

HOWARD WIAL

CENTER FOR URBAN ECONOMIC DEVELOPMENT AND

DEPARTMENT OF URBAN PLANNING AND POLICY,

UNIVERSITY OF ILLINOIS AT CHICAGO

After a decade of the most precipitous manufacturing job loss in U.S. history, the nation is slowly regaining manufacturing jobs. With those recent gains has come a renewed interest in manufacturing among federal, state, and local policymakers and the news media. Much of that interest centers around "advanced manufacturing," a concept that has no precise, widely accepted definition but that generally refers to the use of advanced technologies in the manufacturing process or the creation of new products using those technologies. For example, according to the President's Council of Advisors on Science and Technology, "Advanced manufacturing is a family of activities that (a) depend on the use and coordination of information, automation, computation, software, sensing, and networking, and/or (b) make use of cutting edge materials and emerging capabilities enabled by the physical and biological sciences, for example nanotechnology, chemistry, and biology. It involves both new ways to manufacture existing products, and the manufacture of new products emerging from new advanced technologies."[1] Advanced technologies are also central for the MIT Task Force on Production in the Innovation Economy, which defines advanced manufacturing as "the creation of sustainable capabilities to make successive generations of integrated solutions coupling physical artifacts with services and software".[2] Journalistic accounts of emerging manufacturing technologies have also become common in the news media.[3]

New manufacturing technologies do not exist in a spatial vacuum. American manufacturing is overwhelmingly located in metropolitan areas, and high-technology manufacturing even more so.[4] The assembly line, internal combustion engine, and automobile helped shape the spatial structure of the mid- and late twentieth-century metropolis, with its large factories on large parcels of land, separation of residential and industrial land uses, and auto-dependent sprawl. Similarly, emerging manufacturing technologies, the goods produced using those technologies, and public policies that promote the use of those technologies and their products are likely to influence the spatial development of metropolitan areas in the twenty-first century. Yet the nature of that influence has received virtually no attention from analysts of either manufacturing or metropolitan development.

To be sure, there are some hints in the scholarly and journalistic literature about potential spatial impacts of emerging manufacturing technologies. An extreme view of one of the new technologies, additive manufacturing (also known as 3-D printing), is that it could represent "Wal-Mart in the palm of your hand."[5] Just as paper-and-ink printers are geographically ubiquitous, this view suggests, manufacturing could become something that almost anyone could do almost anywhere; in effect, there could be a factory in every home. The MIT Task Force presents a more nuanced view of the potential of the emerging technologies, arguing that they have the potential to open up new opportunities for small and medium-sized manufacturers, especially those located near customers and nonmanufacturing suppliers, and to reduce the importance of large manufacturers and large factories.[6]

Any discussion of the spatial impacts of emerging manufacturing technologies is inevitably speculative because no data are available to analyze the spatial impacts of technologies that are still very new. However, it is possible to speculate systematically about the potential impacts by combining economic theories of location and land use with descriptions of the new technologies. That is the contribution that this chapter makes. It begins with a brief survey of the technologies. It then lays out an economic framework for conceptualizing their potential spatial impacts, applies that framework to the technologies, and concludes by suggesting public policies that could improve the economic development and workforce impacts of the technologies on metropolitan areas. The chapter emphasizes the use of new manufacturing technologies rather than the (more geographically limited) production of the ideas, materials, machines, and other components that make up the technologies.

This chapter does not argue that manufacturing technologies will be the dominant influence on metropolitan development in the twenty-first century. Because manufacturing accounts for a much smaller share of employment in the United States today than it did in the twentieth century, the spatial impacts of the new technologies may be less profound than those of the assembly line and the automobile. Yet changes in manufacturing technologies could nevertheless exert an outsized influence on metropolitan development because factories are larger—physically and in terms of employment—than other business establishments and because the locations of manufacturers are likely to affect the locations of households and of the many service firms that are linked to manufacturing.

AN OVERVIEW OF THE TECHNOLOGIES

There have been several recent publications that list and catalogue emerging manufacturing technologies.[7] Each categorizes the technologies in a slightly different way, but there is substantial agreement among them about the general nature of the technologies. This section draws on these reports but selects only those technologies that are likely to have a spatial impact. It includes both technologies that are unique to manufacturing and those that are more generally applicable but that have important manufacturing applications. It includes only new manufacturing processes and new products whose primary use will be in those processes, not new manufactured products (such as self-driving cars) whose primary users will be households or nonmanufacturing businesses. It begins with technologies that, according to technical experts, are most likely to be adopted widely in the near future and moves on to those whose adoption is likely to be more distant, less widespread, or more uncertain.

Advanced Sensing and Process Control

Sensors attached to or embedded in objects are currently used in both manufacturing and nonmanufacturing contexts to collect data about the object's location and use automatically. For example, global positioning systems found in most smartphones collect information about how and when the phone is used. In manufacturing and logistics, radio-frequency identification tags are used to track the movement of goods on the assembly line and through the warehouse. Advanced sensing and process control generalizes this kind of tracking to every stage of the production and delivery processes, from raw material to finished product in the factory and from the factory to the consumer (which may be another factory, a nonmanufacturing business, or a household), down to the level of individual pallets and even parts. This is accomplished by placing small sensors on pallets or individual parts, enabling the object to be tracked from the beginning of the supply chain to the end user. In this way, manufacturers can quickly adjust deliveries and production schedules, cutting inefficiencies and improving responsiveness to changes in demand. The technologies required to accomplish these goals are already being used commercially (e.g., General Electric already operates factories in which it monitors the entire production process within the factory via sensors on every pallet and machine), and the costs of the sensors have already begun to decline and are expected to drop further in the near future. For these reasons, both the MIT Task Force and the McKinsey Global Institute consider advanced sensing and process control to be among the technologies most likely to have a substantial impact on production within the next five to ten years.[8]

Cloud Computing

Cloud computing refers to the storage and processing of data and the storage of software on remote servers rather than on on-site hardware. The remote servers are housed on massive server farms run by firms such as Google and Amazon, which rent out space to store data and run applications. Computer users in general are beginning to make the transition from on-site to cloud computing, spurred in part by the lower cost of storing massive amounts of data ("big data") remotely as compared to on-site. Cloud computing is expected to become an integral part of the supply chain and of in-house manufacturing processes, facilitating manufacturers' ability to collect, store, and analyze large amounts of data about their production processes. The McKinsey Global Institute estimates that cloud computing will have a large impact on manufacturers' productivity by 2025.[9]

Industrial Robotics

Although industrial robots have long been used to perform tasks that are too dangerous, difficult, or impractical for humans, they have been too unwieldy to perform tasks that require a high degree of precision. However, the next generation of advanced robotics is beginning to overcome these limitations by creating robots that have greater dexterity, mobility, flexibility, and adaptability. These robots are even capable of working safely side by side with humans and learning from them, enabling a wide potential range of applications. An example is Baxter, a $22,000 human-sized robot introduced in 2012 by Rethink Robotics, a startup company.[10] Baxter is easily trainable to mimic the actions of production workers, is safe enough to work next to humans, and dexterous enough to perform many tactile functions. Because it is neither very fast nor very precise, though, it is most likely to be used for simple, repetitive tasks. Both the MIT Task Force and the McKinsey Global Institute deem robotics likely to have a substantial impact on production within the next five to ten years.[11]

Modular Pharmaceutical Manufacturing

Pharmaceutical manufacturers currently build a new physical and research structure from the ground up for most new drugs. In a new modular approach to pharmaceutical manufacturing, they would instead develop a set of small programmable factories that could be reconfigured for each new drug production run, providing them with more flexibility and real-time monitoring capability. The new modular factories would resemble a set of standardized parts that manufacturers could rearrange to research and produce dugs based on their specific requirements.

Benefits from this development include more efficient manufacturing of "blockbuster" drugs but also possibilities to produce so-called "orphan" drugs that are currently too expensive to manufacture in small production runs.[12] The modular factories could be reusable permanent facilities. Or they could be much smaller, the size of a shipping container, and could be transported anywhere in the world. The latter could not handle complex, experimental drugs, but would have the advantages of low fixed costs, standardization, ease of transport, and ability to be scaled up or down.[13] The MIT Task Force considers modular pharmaceutical production likely to have a substantial impact on the way drugs are produced within the next five to ten years.[14]

Advanced Materials

Advanced materials have novel internal structures that yield superior properties and facilitate transformative changes in manufactured products. Examples include odor-eliminating fibers in socks; stronger, lighter composite metals for airplane fuselages; "smart materials" that are self-cleaning or self-repairing, and nanomaterials.[15] Nanomaterials are those that are manipulated at the molecular level to produce those novel structures and superior properties. They include nanoparticles, usually metals, which are used to deliver targeted cancer drugs, and very lightweight nanocarbon materials such as graphene, which can weigh one-sixth as much as steel per volume, yet be a hundred times as strong. The MIT Task Force assigns very different estimates of potential impact to different kinds of advanced materials.[16] Some materials, such as composites for aircraft, are already in common use, while others (e.g., graphene) are very expensive and are many years away from widespread commercial use.

Digital Manufacturing

Digital manufacturing refers to the increased use of information technology (IT), including software and the Internet, to reduce costs and increase throughput in the entire manufacturing process. For example, design, prototyping, and testing of products are currently distinct operations. A product is designed, a prototype is produced according to that design, and the prototype is tested. If the prototype cannot be produced, or if it does not function as it was designed to, then the process has to begin anew, with another round of design, prototyping, and testing. These operations have to be iterated until the prototype matches and functions according to the design. Digital manufacturing promises to eliminate the need for this iteration by enabling design, virtual prototyping, and virtual testing to be carried out electronically in a single operation, with a physical product produced only after it has been determined electronically that the product matches and functions according to the design.

As another example, digital manufacturing promises to permit computer control of the entire production processes, not only within a factory but across the entire supply chain. This application of digital manufacturing would complement the use of advanced sensors by further automating the production process. It would require manufacturers to collect and analyze of massive amounts of production data to discover patterns in supply usage, delivery times, etc., that would enable them to eliminate inefficiencies and increase response times.

Digital manufacturing also has specific applications to other emerging manufacturing technologies, particularly advanced materials and bio- and pharmaceutical manufacturing. These applications require the development of electronic databases on the properties of materials and human cell functions, respectively. The information in these databases would then be used to design, model, and test new products electronically.[17]

Different aspects of digital manufacturing are likely to be adopted at different rates. Some of the technologies that underlie digital manufacturing (e.g., computer simulation modeling and the analysis of "big data") are already in widespread use and their costs are declining rapidly, but others (such as virtual testing) are still in their infancy and are very costly.

Additive Manufacturing

Additive manufacturing, also known as 3-D printing, is a process in which goods are manufactured by building them up from a series of layers of material rather than by the currently dominant methods of cutting and bending materials. A solid object's specifications are first scanned into a digital file. Next, a software program creates a digital image of the object by "slicing" it digitally into cross sections. The program then sends the image to a 3-D printer. The 3-D printer sprays a plastic or metal resin in successive layers that correspond to the computer image, just as an inkjet printer sprays ink on paper to correspond to a computer image. As each layer is laid down, an ultraviolet light hardens the resin. This process can produce a finished product quickly, often in less than an hour. Plastic resins are currently the materials most commonly used in additive manufacturing but recent advances in powdered metals may enable printing of more complex objects. The materials used for printed objects are likely to weigh less than the metals commonly used today to make many manufactured goods. In addition, because the amount of material it requires to begin making a product is the same as the amount embodied in the finished product, additive manufacturing requires less material input than manufacturing processes that rely on cutting and bending. It also produces no scrap material. An important limitation of additive manufacturing is that it is limited to objects made of at most a small number of materials that can be sprayed independently of one another.

Some manufacturers currently use additive manufacturing for rapid prototyping. Prototypes can be produced in hours instead of days, and without the expensive reconfiguration of tools and dyes with each iterative change. In addition, 3-D printers are slowly coming to be used in larger production runs for test marketing in which multiple prototypes can easily be produced and tested. Eventually, households and businesses of all kinds may own 3-D printers, downloading the designs for a desired object and printing the product themselves, just as they now print documents with paper-and-ink printers. However, their use of 3-D printers is likely to be limited to relatively small objects made of a single type of material. The spread of additive manufacturing will depend on the rate at which the currently very high cost of 3-D printers declines. The MIT Task Force believes that additive manufacturing will have only marginal impacts on production within the next five to ten years, although its panel of experts expressed widely divergent views on the timing of the technology's adoption and the McKinsey Global Institute has a more optimistic view.[18]

A CONCEPTUAL FRAMEWORK

The impacts of these technologies could come about via the locational and land-use decisions of manufacturers, nonmanufacturing businesses, and households, and via the public policies that influence those decisions. Economic theories of location and land use provide a starting point for assessing the potential impacts. These theories suggest that there are five important factors that will shape the impacts.

Agglomeration Economies

An important determinant of the location of economic activities is the presence of agglomeration economies—productivity or cost advantages that accrue to firms by virtue of their location in close proximity to other economic activities in the same industry or in other industries. A new technology that increases these advantages for manufacturers will lead manufacturers to locate near the activities that generate the advantages. These location decisions may give rise to geographic clustering of manufacturing industries or groups of related industries. They may also lead manufacturers to locate in large metropolitan areas or in metropolitan areas more generally.[19] Conversely, a new technology that reduces the productivity or cost advantages of colocation will make industry clustering or metropolitan location less useful to manufacturers, inducing them to spread out geographically. Economists traditionally identify three major sources of agglomeration economies.[20]

First, companies may colocate because they share a common need for workers with a particular set of skills. The various technologies that go into the production of an automobile, for example, create a need for auto and auto parts manufacturers to locate in places where large pools of mechanical engineers and auto-specialized production workers are available. Other manufacturing industries (e.g., machinery manufacturing) requiring similarly skilled workers locate in many of the same regions where auto companies are found.[21] Likewise, a new technology that creates a demand on the part of manufacturers for skills that are not geographically ubiquitous will lead manufacturers to locate in places where those skills are plentiful. (Educational and workforce development policies, therefore, can affect the location of manufacturers by influencing the geography of skill supply.) A technology that reduces manufacturers' need for skilled workers or increases their need for workers whose skills are geographically ubiquitous will make geographic agglomeration less important for manufacturers.

Companies may also locate near one another because they share a need for proximity to specialized suppliers or customers (including private-sector suppliers or customers in service industries as well as those in manufacturing). In the auto industry, the location of suppliers within a day's drive of the assemblers to whom they sell creates cost advantages for both.[22] In many manufacturing industries, the colocation of production and research and development is critical to the quality of both of these activities.[23] Because the need for geographic linkage between production and R&D is likely to be especially strong for early-stage technologies,[24] many new technologies are likely during their initial stage of development to require manufacturers to locate their factories near R&D facilities and therefore, near one another. Because of historical lock-in,[25] these patterns of colocation pay persist even after a technology has matured.[26] A technology may also create a strong long-term need for geographic agglomeration by manufacturers that use it. For example, a recent trend in advanced manufacturing is for producers to supply their customers with both products and maintenance and repair services for those products.[27] If maintenance and repair workers need to have close contact with the factories that make the products, then those factories may benefit from being located near the customers.

The idea of agglomeration based on shared needs for proximity to specialized suppliers may be extended to include proximity to other resources that are not geographically ubiquitous, such as freight transportation facilities (Interstate highways, rail lines, and airports) and public or quasi-public R&D centers (including those at universities). If a new technology is developed at an R&D center and if proximity to the center confers a productive advantage on manufacturers who use the technology (e.g., because manufacturers located near the center learn about the latest technological developments more quickly than other firms), then manufacturers may cluster in locations near the center. If a new technology (such as just-in-time production, which minimizes manufacturers' on-site inventories) makes proximity to a freight transportation facility more necessary or more advantageous, then such a facility can, likewise, be a focal point for a cluster of manufacturers.

The final major source of agglomeration economies is informal face-to-face communication of ideas between skilled workers in different companies.[28] Interfirm sharing of ideas by people working on a common set of problems produces a shared but uncodified understanding of those problems. That understanding benefits all the firms that participate in its development, enabling them to find new ways of improving productivity or cutting costs or making it possible for them to create new products or production processes.

Even in this era of electronic communication, such an understanding can be developed and advanced most effectively through in-person communication, which requires geographic proximity.[29] Silicon Valley, itself a major manufacturing center for computers and advanced electronic products,[30] is perhaps the most prominent contemporary example of a region in which the spillover of ideas between IT firms benefits all those firms.[31] As with geographic linkage of production and R&D, the advantage of interfirm idea sharing is perhaps greatest when a technology is new, but it can also persist even as the technology matures because of historical lock-in and place-specific social relationships among skilled workers.

In addition to these traditional sources of agglomeration economies, Cortright suggests that entrepreneurship may be most likely in regions with preexisting clusters of firms in a particular industry or set of related industries because entrepreneurs in such regions can benefit from the preexisting industry-specific knowledge and supporting institutions that are present there.[32] The same may be true of regions that specialize in a particular technology. In their early stages, radically new technologies are often developed by entrepreneurs who start their own companies.[33] For example, the early decades of the twentieth century, when auto manufacturing was a new industry, were characterized by a proliferation of small auto manufacturers in the Detroit area.[34] Even as a technology matures, it may continue to support high levels of entrepreneurship, and the high levels of geographic agglomeration that accompany them, if it does not give rise to substantial economies of scale. Advanced-technology athletic goods manufacturing in Portland (Oregon), optics and photonics in Rochester (New York), and medical device manufacturing in Minneapolis are examples; despite the presence of large firms in the relevant industries in these regions, each region supports a robust community of newer small firms even though the underlying technologies are no longer new.[35]

Regardless of their source, agglomeration economies that make manufacturers more productive also benefit the employees of those companies. Manufacturing workers in an industry that is strongly concentrated in a particular metropolitan area receive higher wages than those who work in the same industry in metropolitan areas where that industry is less concentrated.[36] Thus, any new manufacturing technology that encourages the geographic agglomeration of manufacturers is also likely to raise the wages of manufacturing workers in the places where those manufacturers are most concentrated. Conversely, any new manufacturing technology that encourages the geographic dispersion of factories is likely to lower wages.

Amenity Values

Geographic variations in productivity and costs influence the location of manufacturing facilities by affecting the value that manufacturers place on particular geographic locations. Similarly, the presence or absence of place-specific amenities (such as a clean and pleasant physical environment) influences the location of households by affecting the value households place on particular locations, especially locations within a given metropolitan area. If a new manufacturing technology gives rise to large, dirty, unsightly plants that generate large amounts of truck traffic, then residents will want to move away from those plants. Higher-income residents will be willing and able to afford to pay the most to live far from the plants, and those households will be more concentrated in neighborhoods where manufacturers are less concentrated. The residential undesirability of locations near the plants is likely to create a demand (once again, most prominent among high-income residents) for zoning ordinances that separate residences from manufacturing plants. New manufacturing technologies that enable smaller, less-polluting plants requiring less truck traffic to transport their products will have the opposite impacts on residential location: there will be more geographic mixing, or at least less extreme geographic separation, of residences and manufacturing plants; higher-income residents will be willing to live closer to plants (although not necessarily next door to them); and zoning ordinances will be less likely to require strict separation of manufacturing from residential uses. (For example, form-based zoning codes, which regulate land uses on the basis of physical form rather than on the basis of type of use, may become more common as such technologies spread.)

Having a more pleasant factory as a neighbor, of course, does not constitute a free lunch for residents. If households are not willing to pay as much to live far from factories, then locations near factories will have higher housing prices than they do at present.[37] Low-income residents who currently live near factories may be displaced by higher-income households. The presence of manufacturing plants in a neighborhood may become a cause of, rather than a barrier to, gentrification and displacement of the poor. Although the highest-income residents may not want to live near even the cleanest, quietest factories, middle- and lower-middle-income residents may displace poorer residents from neighborhoods that are home to manufacturing establishments.

Transportation Costs

The cost of transporting goods (raw materials, components, and finished goods) affects the location of manufacturing plants. If transportation costs are very high, then manufacturers will spread out geographically to locate near their customers. As transportation costs fall, it is less important for manufacturers to locate near their customers and agglomeration economies will outweigh the dispersive force of transportation costs, leading manufacturers to cluster together (in industry- or technology-specific clusters and/ or large metropolitan areas). However, large concentrations of people and firms create costs in the form of congestion and pollution. If transportation costs fall even further in a world where geographic clustering is important, then companies will once again spread out geographically—in Thomas Friedman's terminology, the world will become "flat."[38] Thus, a new manufacturing technology that reduced transportation costs would be likely to cause manufacturers—who are currently strongly concentrated in particular U.S. metropolitan areas[39]—to become more geographically dispersed.

A manufacturing technology could affect freight transportation costs in two ways. First, it could help create new modes of transportation with new cost structures. For example, the internal combustion engine, along with other technologies, enabled the creation of the truck, which is less expensive than the railroad for shipping freight over relatively short distances.

A new manufacturing technology could also affect freight transportation costs by altering the weight-to-value ratio of manufactured goods. A technology that facilitated the creation of lighter-weight products (while raising or leaving unchanged the value of each unit produced) would reduce the cost of shipping each unit, enabling manufacturers to locate further from their suppliers and customers. For example, the use of aluminum, plastic, or lightweight composites in place of steel in autos could have this effect.

Plant-Level Scale Economies

Manufacturing technologies can affect manufacturers' land use decisions as well as their location choices. The physically integrated nature of much manufacturing, especially that conducted on assembly lines, makes large plants more economical than smaller ones for many types of production. In the early twentieth century these plant-level economies of scale led manufacturers to build large, multistory factories. After World War II, they (along with the substitution of trucking for rail as the primary means of shipping products) meant that factories were most economically built as sprawling single-story facilities on large plots of land. (Because land is less expensive in smaller metropolitan areas and nonmetropolitan areas and far from the city center in any metropolitan area, this land use requirement also induced manufacturers to locate their factories accordingly.) New manufacturing technologies that increase economies of scale may lead to the continuation or acceleration of these late-twentieth-century trends, while those that reduce scale economies could reverse them. If new technologies reduce scale economies, then factories could be located on smaller parcels of land, which would make more centralized locations in larger metropolitan areas more economical than they were in the past.

Input Requirements

Technological change can affect the intensity with which manufacturers use different productive inputs, such as labor, land, and machinery. Perhaps the most important example of this is automation, which has been a long-term trend in manufacturing. Labor-intensive production processes will lead to the creation of large numbers of jobs in each factory, while more automated processes may mean that relatively large factories have relatively few workers. The labor intensity of production, therefore, has implications for land use planning.

The greatest recent public-policy concern, however, has focused on the implications of automation for overall levels of manufacturing employment. Manufacturers' increasing use of highly automated factories has led some observers to predict that manufacturing employment will decline in the future even if manufacturers "reshore" substantial amounts of production to the United States.[40] Brynjolfsson and McAfee generalize this reasoning beyond manufacturing, arguing that the substitution of computer technologies for workers in all sectors of the economy will cause a long-term decline in virtually all types of employment.[41] However, although this possibility cannot be ruled out, either for manufacturing or for the U.S. economy as a whole, it is not inevitable and, thus far, is not supported by empirical evidence. Mechanization reduces the amount of labor required to make each unit of a product but, at the same time, reduces the cost of producing each unit, thereby expanding the market for the product and, with it, the total number of workers needed. Whether the net impact of mechanization is to reduce or expand employment depends on which of these two effects is larger. The available evidence suggests that more rapid productivity growth in U.S. manufacturing (which is often achieved through automation) has been associated with job growth (or, during periods of manufacturing job loss, with a reduction in the rate of job loss) rather than with more rapid job loss.[42]

Mechanization may have other positive impacts for manufacturing workers as well. Manufacturers who use labor less intensively will be less concerned about labor costs when locating production facilities. The ongoing interstate and interregional competition for manufacturing will depend less on labor costs. Low-wage locations, whether domestic or foreign, will exert less downward pressure on manufacturing wages in high-wage U.S. regions. The productivity growth that mechanization creates would also be expected to raise the wages of manufacturing workers. However, the evidence suggests that high plant-level productivity is less closely linked to high wages than it was in the past.[43] Moreover, economy-wide, the U.S. median hourly wage has not come close to keeping pace with productivity growth since the 1970s.[44] Therefore, it seems unlikely that the productivity gains from mechanization will translate into equivalent wage gains for manufacturing workers in the absence of public policies that raise wages directly.

Depending on the specifics of each technology, the above channels of impact may occur at various geographic scales. Some new technologies may influence the distribution of manufacturing facilities and jobs between the United States and other nations. Others may influence the distribution of manufacturing activity between metropolitan and nonmetropolitan areas of the United States, between large and small metropolitan areas, or within individual metropolitan areas. Some may have substantial impacts on metropolitan areas that currently specialize in particular manufacturing industries or technologies while mattering little for other regions.

Time horizons also affect impacts. The impacts of new manufacturing technologies may occur at different speeds depending in part on the rate at which manufacturers adopt them. The impacts of any given technology may also be different in its earliest stages of commercial adoption than in its more mature phases. For example, agglomeration economies based on the advantages of face-to-face communication or close proximity between factories and R&D labs may weaken somewhat as a technology matures.

IMPACTS ON METROPOLITAN DEVELOPMENT

The channels of impact on metropolitan development differ substantially by technology. Additive manufacturing and digital manufacturing have the potential for the most far-reaching impacts, but those impacts are not likely to occur on a large scale within the next decade, if ever. Impacts of other technologies will be narrower but more likely to occur in a relatively short period of time.

Additive Manufacturing: A Factory in Every Home?

Additive manufacturing has the potential to operate through all the above channels of impact. Its lower material requirements will reduce scale economies, enabling factories and manufacturing firms to be smaller. The opportunities that additive manufacturing creates for smaller companies may make manufacturing more likely to be located in metropolitan areas, especially large ones, since those places have the supporting institutions that new entrepreneurs need.

The smaller factories will require less land than conventional factories, enabling them to locate in denser metropolitan centers. Their absence of industrial waste and relatively quiet production processes could make them less undesirable as neighbors to households and to a wide variety of service firms. Residents' demand for zoning that separates industrial from commercial and residential uses could decline.

Overall, additive manufacturing could reduce the number of workers needed to produce an individual unit of a product and, if the technology becomes sufficiently widespread, perhaps even the total number of manufacturing workers. It is also likely to change the mix of workers required. The technology will reduce the demand for machinists, welders, and other workers who currently cut or bend metals, although its restricted ability to combine different materials in a given product will limit the extent of this reduction. Thus, the concentration of those workers in particular regions (e.g., the industrial Midwest) may become a less important influence on the location of production. At the same time, additive manufacturing may increase the demand for industrial designers, who write the computer programs used to print objects. Its use in rapid prototyping may make face-to-face contact between designers and production workers more important, causing production to cluster in places where there are already large concentrations of designers. Those locations are likely to be large metropolitan areas, which include some traditional metalworking and machinery centers (e.g., Detroit, Chicago, and Cleveland) but may include other large metropolitan areas that are currently not manufacturing centers (e.g., New York and San Francisco).

Additive manufacturing also has a strong potential to lead to the disagglomeration of manufacturers that use it. Compared to conventional processes, it requires less material input per unit of finished product and produces lighter-weight products as outputs, thus making transportation costs less important as determinants of manufacturers' locations. The reduced importance of transportation costs reduces the economic value of geographic clustering of any kind. Thus, additive manufacturing could lead to a "flatter world" in which manufacturing could occur almost anywhere. Whether this disagglomerative force is stronger than the agglomerative forces of increased entrepreneurship and face-to-face contact between designers and production workers will determine the net impact of the technology on geographic clusters of manufacturers.

Additive manufacturing is the only one of the currently emerging manufacturing technologies that has the potential to approximate the ideal of "a factory in every home." The potential will never be fully realized, even if 3-D printers become as inexpensive as inkjet printers, because additive manufacturing cannot be used to join together different types of materials and is unlikely to be usable for very large objects. However, the technology is perhaps the most geographically disruptive of all those surveyed in this chapter. It has the potential to create many more opportunities for small manufacturers, especially suppliers of lightweight components. It could also alter existing regional manufacturing specializations, either by reducing the importance of those specializations or by relocating them to new metropolitan areas. Overall, nonmetropolitan areas and small midwestern metropolitan areas that specialize in metal products but lack concentrations of industrial designers may be at risk of losing their manufacturing specializations as the technology spreads. The central cities of large metropolitan areas, on the other hand, could gain manufacturing specializations.

Digital Manufacturing and the MIT Vision

Digital manufacturing is second to additive manufacturing in the scope of its potential impact on metropolitan development. In the short term, its early adopters are likely to be large companies capable of making what are now relatively expensive investments in computer simulation and testing. However, in the long term, as costs decline, digital manufacturing could reduce economies of scale because product design, testing, and access to assemblers and larger suppliers all become less expensive than they are at present. Thus, the technology could open up new opportunities for small suppliers.

Although digital manufacturing will, in principle, increase opportunities for suppliers located far from their customers, it may not increase the geographic dispersion of supply chains by very much, if at all. Just as the spread of electronic communication does not necessarily reduce the importance of geographic proximity for individuals, especially for complex communication,[45] the spread of digital manufacturing will not necessarily make geography less important for suppliers. Even after initial technical problems that impede the smooth operation of digital supply chain relationships are solved, the purely relational aspects of supplier-to-assembler and supplier-to-supplier ties will continue to exist. These depend on face-to-face communication among people in different companies, which will continue to support geographic clustering of companies in the same supply chain. Moreover, because digital manufacturing will reduce or eliminate the substantial time lags that currently exist between design, testing, and prototyping, it will also reduce the cost of customized production. More customized production may lead to more interaction, including more in-person communication, between suppliers' industrial designers and their customers, thereby encouraging more geographic clustering within the supply chain.

As with additive manufacturing, digital manufacturing's reduction of scale economies and opening up of opportunities for small firms may increase the presence of manufacturing in metropolitan areas generally and in large metropolitan areas and their dense cores in particular. In addition, increased needs for in-person interaction between industrial designers and their firms' customers, which results from increased customization, may extend to household as well as business customers. Because households are predominantly located in metropolitan areas, the increased need for in-person communication between designers and customers could be an additional force for the increased metropolitanization of manufacturing.

The technology's integration of design, testing, and prototyping is likely to increase the demand for skilled production technicians who have a combination of skills in computer programming, data analysis, machine operation, and assembly. If this combination of skills is not geographically ubiquitous, manufacturers using digital technology may cluster in locations with large concentrations of these workers. Because the necessary skills include both production skills that are currently common in established manufacturing-based regions and IT and data analysis skills that are currently common in IT centers, both types of metropolitan areas could become centers for the early adopters of digital technology. Metropolitan areas that already have concentrations of both types of workers, such as Rochester, New York, may have an initial advantage as a location for digital manufacturers.

Although digital manufacturing has no direct impact on the cost of freight transportation, the spread of this technology could place pressure on governments to upgrade highways, railroads, and airports. Digital manufacturing promises to speed up the production process by integrating what are now distinct stages within that process and by reducing the cost of communication between manufacturer and manufacturer and between manufacturer and household consumer If it succeeds in doing so, then inefficiencies in the freight transportation system will account for a larger share of combined production and distribution costs. Reduction or elimination of these inefficiencies could then become a more important policy priority. Although the inefficiencies anywhere in the national and international freight transportation network could affect the speed of the production-distribution process, inefficiencies that exist near manufacturers may be especially salient to them. Therefore, digital manufacturing may induce manufacturers to locate in places with better freight transportation access.

Digital manufacturing does not have the potential to encourage geographic disagglomeration to the extent that additive manufacturing, in its most extreme form, could. It will not eliminate existing manufacturing clusters in metropolitan areas that also have concentrations of IT workers. Even if fully implemented, it will not replace any part of manufacturing with home-based production. Instead, it seems more suited to realize the MIT Task Force's vision of a more "democratized" manufacturing sector in which small and medium-sized sized firms, especially those located near their suppliers and their business and household customers, become the dominant players in manufacturing.[46] This ideal, though, is not likely to be realized within the next decade because the technical obstacles to the full implementation of digital manufacturing, as well as the obstacles created by inefficiencies in the transportation system, will remain substantial.

Advanced Sensing

Advanced sensing will probably have some but not all of digital manufacturing's impacts, and these impacts will likely occur sooner because advanced sensing is already beginning to be applied commercially. Large firms that currently move large quantities of manufactured goods through their factories will probably be the earliest adopters of advanced sensing. However, as the costs of sensors fall, this technology could become increasingly accessible to small firms. Eventually it could erode the advantage that large firms currently have in tracking their products, thereby reducing once source of scale economies. Like additive and digital manufacturing, advanced sensing will ultimately be a force for smaller factories, which may be more likely to be located in metropolitan areas and especially in denser parts of those areas.

Advanced sensing will increase the demand for logistics specialists and technicians who are experts in analyzing the large amounts of data that advanced sensors produce. If these workers are not geographically ubiquitous, then manufacturers may cluster in places where there are large concentrations of them.

Like digital manufacturing, advanced sensing will remove inefficiencies in the movement of goods through and between factories and from factories to household consumers. It could, therefore, lead manufacturers to place a premium on more efficient freight transportation systems. Manufacturers using advanced sensing may locate in places with better transportation access and may advocate for public investment in improved freight transportation.

Advanced Materials

The manufacturers of advanced materials are likely to locate near sources of R&D, including universities that research such materials. As the markets for these materials grow, their manufacturers will increase their employment of materials scientists and engineers.

The most important impacts of advanced materials on firms that use them will probably come through transportation costs. Because these materials are lighter than the conventional materials that they replace, firms using advanced materials will manufacture products that are lighter in relation to their value than firms using conventional materials. The resulting decline in the importance of transportation costs as a factor in manufacturers' location decisions will weaken existing geographic concentrations of manufacturers, making them more footloose and giving them less reason to locate in metropolitan areas, especially large metropolitan areas. Reinforcing this impact will be the increasing use of lightweight materials in the trucks, ships, and aircraft that are used to ship manufactured products of all kinds. The lighter vehicles will use less fuel per ton-mile of products shipped, reducing transportation costs and, therefore, reducing agglomeration economies for manufacturers generally.

A second impact of advanced materials may come from the largely unknown health impacts of these materials. To the extent that these materials pose major health risks, households and other businesses will pay a premium to locate far from the factories that use the materials and the places where the materials are recycled or disposed of. This will reinforce the existing demand for zoning that segregates manufacturers from households and most service businesses. If labor markets are sufficiently tight, then firms using dangerous advanced materials will have to pay their workers a wage premium.

Industrial Robotics

Large companies are currently the major users of industrial robots, but as robots become smaller and less expensive they will be increasingly accessible to smaller manufacturers. This will weaken one source of scale economies. Like most of the other emerging manufacturing technologies, therefore, robotics will ultimately make small and medium-sized manufacturers more competitive with larger ones. The result, as with other technologies that have this effect, is likely to be a shift of manufacturing toward smaller pieces of land located in metropolitan areas in general and in large metropolitan areas and their dense core areas in particular.

As with other kinds of industrial automation, robotics will reduce the labor content of each unit of manufactured product but, as noted previously, its impact on overall manufacturing employment is uncertain. The spread of robotics will increase manufacturers' demand for two specific kinds of workers: the engineers who design the robots and the factories in which they are used and the technicians who install, maintain, and repair the robots. If those workers are not geographically ubiquitous, manufacturers who use robots may cluster in metropolitan areas with concentrations of those workers. Because the required engineering and technical skills are similar to those already found in metropolitan areas that specialize in the production of machinery, transportation equipment, and metal products, those metropolitan areas may be the locations most attractive to manufacturers that use robots and they may also be the ones in which the increased demands for engineers and robotics technicians are most concentrated.

Cloud Computing

As cloud computing spreads, large manufacturers will no longer need to house servers at or near their facilities, and they will no longer need to store software or hire many IT specialists. Thus, they will be able to reduce the size of their factories, R&D centers, and headquarters to some extent. Without the need to build or rent their own IT infrastructure or hire their own IT staff, smaller manufacturers will also enjoy reduced computing costs. Thus, cloud computing will weaken one source of scale economies. In so doing, it will create more opportunities for small manufacturers, who are more likely than their larger counterparts to locate in metropolitan areas, large metropolitan areas, and dense core areas of large metropolitan areas.

Cloud computing could be a force for geographic disagglomeration of manufacturing, although its impact on agglomeration, if any, is likely to be small. Because manufacturers will no longer need to hire many IT specialists, they will be less likely to cluster in places where those workers are concentrated. Cloud computing will facilitate virtual collaboration between manufacturing workers and their firms' customers, suppliers, and offsite R&D workers. This could be a disagglomerative force if virtual collaboration becomes a very good substitute for in-person collaboration. However, much of the need for collaboration in manufacturing revolves around the need to see and manipulate machines and physical products. Virtual collaboration may eventually be possible even for those activities, but this development is probably far in the future.

Modular Pharmaceutical Manufacturing

This technology will permit a reduction in the size of pharmaceutical factories and will eliminate the need to build new factories for many new drugs. Both of these changes will cause modest reductions in scale economies and probably in pharmaceutical manufacturers' total land consumption. However, without changes in the pharmaceutical research and development system, they will not create opportunities for smaller firms to enter the industry because only large firms will be able to afford the substantial R&D investments needed to introduce new drugs. Nor is the reduction in land consumption likely to be sufficient to induce pharmaceutical companies to move their plants from suburban and exurban campuses to dense metropolitan cores. Within the suburbs and exurbs where pharmaceutical companies are currently located, though, those companies will require less land.

The possibility of shipping entire pharmaceutical plants to new locations is likely to intensify the already substantial interregional and international tax competition for pharmaceutical manufacturing.[47] Because pharmaceutical companies will still need to locate their plants in close proximity to sources of R&D, however, this competition will continue to be limited to a relatively small number of metropolitan areas that already have very strong pharmaceutical specializations. In the United States, there are fifty-two such metropolitan areas, the largest of which are New York, Chicago, Philadelphia, Boston, San Francisco, and Indianapolis.[48]

Although the potential impacts of the technologies are quite diverse, following are some common patterns.

- All the technologies except advanced materials and modular pharmaceutical manufacturing are likely to reduce scale economies sufficiently to create new opportunities for small and medium-sized manufacturers, while none of them has any long-term potential to increase scale economies.

- On balance, this will probably result in larger shares of manufacturers and manufacturing jobs being located in metropolitan areas, large metropolitan areas, and dense metropolitan cores; the incentives for disagglomeration that are present in additive manufacturing, digital manufacturing, advanced materials, and cloud computing will probably not be strong enough, at least within the next decade, to counteract these tendencies.

- Except for additive manufacturing, none of the technologies is likely to make manufacturers more pleasant neighbors for households or many service firms. Therefore, the technologies will not, on balance, be a force for the integration of residential and commercial land uses with manufacturing within metropolitan areas.

- Digital manufacturing, advanced sensing, and robotics will create a demand for new kinds of skilled production and maintenance/repair technicians, while only additive manufacturing has the potential for large-scale deskilling of manufacturing jobs, and that potential is not likely to be realized in the next decade, if ever. The presence of those workers could be a magnet for the creation of new regional clusters of manufacturers and the continued strength of existing clusters in regions that develop education and training programs for the new skills.

- Digital manufacturing and advanced sensing could make location near high-quality freight transportation facilities a more important locational factor for manufacturers. This could also be true to a lesser extent for other technologies that accelerate the production process, such as additive manufacturing, robotics, and cloud computing.

PUBLIC-POLICY IMPLICATIONS

State, metropolitan, and local policy makers should harness the potential of the new manufacturing technologies to support "high-road" economic development strategies. Such strategies accentuate the economic benefits of geographic agglomeration and require highly paid skilled workers (including production workers) who use their skills to help their employers innovate and become more productive.[49] To maximize the new technologies' potential to support the high road, public policies are needed in five major areas:

research and development, technical assistance to small and medium-sized manufacturers, pro-manufacturing zoning, education and workforce development to train the next generation of skilled manufacturing technicians, and public investment in improved freight transportation. Public policy should also discourage "low-road" strategies that depend heavily on low wages and relocation incentives that fuel the interjurisdictional competition for manufacturers.

Research and Development

The emerging technologies are likely to increase small and medium-sized firms' shares of manufacturing firms and output, placing more responsibility for manufacturing innovation in the hands of those firms. However, with the exception of startup companies spun off from university labs, these manufacturers do very little R&D.[50] Therefore, the growing role of small and medium-sized companies in manufacturing may threaten the nation's ability to innovate.

Manufacturing innovation centers, supported by public and matching private funds, could help solve this problem. These centers should help small and medium-sized manufacturers innovate by working on the applied R&D problems most important to those manufacturers.[51] Each center should focus on a technology of special importance to a metropolitan area or broader region. Each center could be a focal point for the creation of a new cluster of small and medium-sized manufacturers that use the technology in which the center specializes. These clusters could be long-lasting if the regions in which they are located gain a head start in the development of their respective technologies.

The centers that constitute the federal government's National Network for Manufacturing Innovation provide a model for a national network of such centers. At the metropolitan level, the state-funded, university-based advanced materials research centers in Upstate New York (especially Albany) and the privately funded semiconductor research consortium Sematech provide additional models.[52]

Technical Assistance

Small and medium-sized manufacturers often lag in other practices that support innovation, such as adopting methods of work organization and business organization that improve productivity. The federal-state Manufacturing Extension Partnership (MEP) Program currently assists small and medium-sized manufacturers on a voluntary fee-for-service basis with the adoption of these practices, as do a few state- and privately supported programs, such as the Center for Integrated Manufacturing Studies at the Rochester Institute of Technology. These programs have some important limitations. They do not meet all the needs that small and medium-sized manufacturers have for technical assistance. Furthermore, they typically provide assistance to all firms that are willing to pay their fees and do not prioritize firms that are most likely to achieve high road outcomes.

To overcome these limitations, all publicly supported technical assistance to manufacturers should be given only to firms that either meet minimum standards on wages, productivity, productivity growth, and innovation, or have government-approved plans to meet such standards within a reasonable time period. In addition, state and local governments should develop supplementary programs that help small and medium-sized manufacturers with the kinds of problems that are beyond the purview of MEP-type programs. For example, New York City helps small businesses, including manufacturers, develop business plans.[53] Through its Local Industrial Retention Initiative, Chicago supports a network of community development organizations that help manufacturers navigate such municipal processes as zoning and permitting and advocate for the needs of manufacturers in their neighborhoods.[54]

Zoning

The growing importance of small and medium-sized manufacturers is likely to increase manufacturers' demand for metropolitan locations, including dense core locations. However, many central cities and inner suburbs either "zone out" manufacturing or leave manufacturers to compete with other land uses, such as retail stores or luxury housing, that generate higher property values. These policies work against the social benefits of manufacturing that are best realized in the more dense parts of metropolitan areas (such as the role that such locations play in promoting innovation and productivity growth in manufacturing) but that are not fully reflected in market-determined property values. To solve this problem, municipalities should create special manufacturing zones in some of their densely developed areas, as Chicago and other cities already have done.[55]

Workforce Development

Education and training programs will be needed to meet the demands for skilled technical workers in manufacturing that many of the emerging technologies are likely to stimulate. Examples of such programs currently in operation include Chicago's Austin Polytechnic Academy (a public high school dedicated to manufacturing) and Pittsburgh's New App for Making It in America (an experimental U.S. Department of Labor–funded multiemployer labor-management apprenticeship program focused on the needs of small, high-tech manufacturers). Programs such as these, if implemented on a large enough scale within a metropolitan area, could help the metropolitan area develop a long-lasting advantage in attracting and retaining manufacturers that intensively use the skills that the programs develop.

Freight Transportation

By accelerating the process of transporting products from suppliers to assemblers to final customers, improved freight transportation would complement the new technologies' potential to accelerate the production process. More public investment in rail (with its environmental benefits) and better maintenance of highways and airports would improve the U.S. freight network. The regions with the best freight hubs could develop a long-lasting advantage in attracting and retaining manufacturers that use the technologies that place the greatest premium on high-quality freight transportation.

Discouraging the Low Road

The new technologies will make labor costs less of a competitive factor in the location of manufacturing, creating greater opportunity for public policies to raise wages directly without driving away manufacturers. At the same time, they will increase the importance of smaller firms in manufacturing, which pay lower wages than larger companies.[56] To help ensure that advanced technologies support high-wage manufacturing jobs, state and federal governments should encourage unionization, avoid right-to-work laws, and provide firm-specific economic development incentives (if at all) only to those manufacturers that either (a) pay high wages and have high levels of productivity and rates of productivity growth and innovation or (b) demonstrate they are likely to do so within a reasonable amount of time. Governments that provide such assistance should have the right to reclaim amounts paid to firms that do not meet these requirements.

State and local governments that eschew low-road competition for manufacturers are not "unilaterally disarming" themselves in their quest for manufacturing jobs. Rather, they are changing the basis on which they compete for manufacturers: from low wages and relocation subsidies to innovation, skilled labor, and high-quality transportation. Cities and states that make this shift will be better able to attract the advanced manufacturers of the future and help their residents secure the location-specific benefits that the new manufacturing technologies promise.

Notes

The author is grateful to Joel Benedetti for research assistance.

1. President's Council of Advisors on Science and Technology, *Report to the President on Capturing Domestic Competitive Advantage in Advanced Manufacturing* (Washington, D.C.: Executive Office of the President, 2012).

2. Suzanne Berger, *Making in America: From Innovation to Market* (Cambridge, Mass.: MIT Press, 2013).

3. See, e.g., Adam Davidson, "Making It in America," *Atlantic*, December 20, 2011, accessed February 11, 2014, www.theatlantic.com/magazine; John Koten, "A Revolution in the Making," *Wall Street Journal*, June 10, 2013, sec. Journal Reports; Paul Markillie, "Manufacturing the Future," *Economist*, November 21, 2012, accessed February 11, 2014, www.economist.com; Alexis Madrigal and Sarah Rich, "The Internet and Things: How Manufacturing Could Get Better with a Dose of Networked Data," *Atlantic*, September 20, 2012, accessed February 11, 2014, www.theatlantic.com/technology.

4. Susan Helper, Timothy Krueger, and Howard Wial, *Locating American Manufacturing: Trends in the Geography of Production* (Washington, D.C.: Brookings Institution, 2012).

5. Elizabeth Royte, "What Lies Ahead for 3-D Printing?," *Smithsonian Magazine*, May 2013, accessed February 11, 2014, www.smithsonianmag.com.

6. Berger, *Making in America*.

7. Ibid.; James Manyika, Michael Chui, Jacques Bughin, Richard Dobbs, Peter Bisson, and Alex Marrs, *Disruptive Technologies: Advances That Will Transform Life, Business, and the Global Economy* (N.p.: McKinsey Global Institute, May 2013); President's Council of Advisors on Science and Technology, *Report*; Stephanie S. Shipp, Nayanee Gupta, Bhavya Lal, Justin A. Scott, Christopher L. Weber, Michael S. Finnin, Meredith Blake, Sherrica Newsome, and Samuel Thomas, *Emerging Global Trends in Advanced Manufacturing* (Alexandria, Va.: Institute for Defense Analyses, 2012).

8. Olivier De Weck, Darci Reed, Sanjay Sarma, and Martin Schmidt, "Trends in Advanced Manufacturing Technology Innovation," in *Production in the Innovation Economy*, edited by Richard M. Locke and Rachel Wellhausen (Cambridge, Mass.: MIT Press, 2014); Manyika et al., *Disruptive Technologies*.

9. Manyika et al., *Disruptive Technologies*.

10. Erico Guizzo and Evan Ackerman, "How Rethink Robotics Built Its New Baxter Robot Worker," *IEEE Spectrum*, September 18, 2012, accessed February 11, 2014, http://spectrum.ieee.org/robotics.

11. De Weck et al., "Trends in Advanced Manufacturing Technology Innovation"; Manyika et al., *Disruptive Technologies*.

12. De Weck et al., "Trends in Advanced Manufacturing Technology Innovation."

13. Paul Thomas, "Modular Construction in Pharma: No Longer a Novelty," *Pharmaceutical Manufacturing Magazine*, January 11, 2012.

14. De Weck et al., "Trends in Advanced Manufacturing Technology Innovation."

15. Manyika et al., *Disruptive Technologies.*

16. De Weck et al., "Trends in Advanced Manufacturing Technology Innovation."

17. Shipp et al., *Emerging Global Trends.*

18. De Weck et al., "Trends in Advanced Manufacturing Technology Innovation"; Manyika et al., *Disruptive Technologies.*

19. Factories that are located in geographic areas with high densities of business establishments (regardless of whether the latter are in manufacturing or not) are more productive than isolated manufacturing establishments. See Marcus Stanley and Susan Helper, "Urbanization and Manufacturing: Are There Ideas in the Air?," working paper, Weatherhead School of Management, Case Western Reserve University, 2006.

20. Alfred Marshall, *Principles of Economics* (London: Macmillan, 1920); Joseph Cortright, *Making Sense of Clusters: Regional Competitiveness and Economic Development* (Washington, D.C.: Brookings Institution, 2006).

21. Helper et al., *Locating American Manufacturing.*

22. Thomas H. Klier and Daniel P. McMillen, "Clustering of Auto Supplier Plants in the United States: Generalized Method of Moments Spatial Logic for Large Samples," *Journal of Business and Economic Statistics* 26, no. 4 (2008): 460–71.

23. Susan Helper, Timothy Krueger, and Howard Wial, *Why Does Manufacturing Matter? Which Manufacturing Matters? A Policy Framework* (Washington, D.C.: Brookings Institution, 2012); Gregory Tassey, "Rationales and Mechanisms for Revitalizing U.S. Manufacturing R&D Strategies," *Journal of Technology Transfer* 35 (2010): 283–333.

24. Gilles Duranton and Diego Puga, "Nursery Cities: Urban Diversity, Process Innovation, and the Life Cycle of Products," *American Economic Review* 91, no. 5 (2001): 1454–77.

25. Cortright, *Making Sense of Clusters.*

26. The maturation of a technology is not simply the result of the exhaustion of the possibilities for applying the technology that occurs with the passage of time. It can also be influenced by business strategies and public policies that enable or impede the development of new applications of an existing technology or of new technologies that emerge from the existing technology. See Michael Storper, *Keys to the City: How Economics, Institutions, Social Interactions, and Politics Shape Development* (Princeton, N.J.: Princeton University Press, 2013).

27. De Weck et al., "Trends in Advanced Manufacturing Technology Innovation."

28. Cortright, *Making Sense of Clusters.*

29. Michael Storper and Anthony Venables, "Buzz: Face-to-Face Contact and the Urban Economy," *Journal of Economic Geography* 4, no. 4 (2004): 351–70.

30. Helper et al., *Locating American Manufacturing.*

31. AnnaLee Saxenian, *Regional Advantage: Culture and Competition in Silicon Valley and Route 128* (Cambridge, Mass.: Harvard University Press, 1994).

32. Cortright, *Making Sense of Clusters.*

33. William J. Baumol, *The Free Market Innovation Machine: Analyzing the Growth Miracle of Capitalism* (Princeton, N.J.: Princeton University Press, 2004).

34. George C. Galster, *Driving Detroit: The Quest for Respect in Motown* (Philadelphia: University of Pennsylvania Press, 2012).

35. Jennifer Clark, *Working Regions: Reconnecting Innovation and Production in the Knowledge Economy* (New York: Routledge, 2013).

36. William C. Wheaton and Mark J. Lewis, "Urban Wages and Labor Market Agglomeration," *Journal of Urban Economics* 51, no. 3 (2002): 542–62.

37. Following Roback, most mainstream urban and regional economic theories also predict that entire metropolitan areas where manufacturing is strongly concentrated will have higher housing prices if factories become less objectionable as neighbors, since households will be willing to pay more to live in those metropolitan areas than they do at present. See Jennifer Roback, "Wages, Rents, and the Quality of Life," *Journal of Political Economy* 90, no. 6 (1982): 1257–78. Storper (*Keys to the City*), however, questions whether such a change in amenity values would initiate the household mobility between metropolitan areas that would be necessary to generate such a change in housing prices.

38. Gianmarco P. Ottaviano and Diego Puga, "Agglomeration in the Global Economy: A Survey of the 'New Economic Geography,'" *World Economy* 21, no. 6 (1998): 707–31; Thomas L. Friedman, *The World Is Flat: A Brief History of the Twenty-First Century* (New York: Farrar, Straus and Giroux, 2005).

39. Helper et al., *Locating American Manufacturing*.

40. Robert J. Samuelson, "The Long Road to 'Full Employment,'" Washingtonpost.com, July 15, 2013, accessed February 11, 2014, www.lexisnexis.com.

41. Erik Brynjolfsson and Andrew McAfee, *Race against the Machine: How the Digital Revolution Is Accelerating Innovation, Driving Productivity, and Irreversibly Transforming Employment and the Economy* (Lexington, Mass.: Digital Frontier Press, 2012).

42. This does not mean that dislocation of workers by machines does not occur (and require more robust income support and workforce development policies than those that have ever existed in the United States). It simply means that mechanization does not necessarily lead to overall losses of manufacturing jobs. Ben Miller and Robert D. Atkinson, *Are Robots Taking Our Jobs, or Making Them?* (Washington, D.C.: Information Technology and Innovation Foundation, 2013); Berger, *Making in America*; Helper et al., *Why Does Manufacturing Matter?*

43. Mark C. Long, Kristin Dziczek, Daniel D. Luria, and Edith A. Wiarda, "Wage and Productivity Stability in U.S. Manufacturing Plants," *Monthly Labor Review*, May 2008, 24–36.

44. Lawrence Mishel and Kar-Fai Gee, "Why Aren't Workers Benefiting from Productivity Growth in the United States?," *International Productivity Monitor* 23 (2012): 31–43.

45. Jess Gaspar and Edward L. Glaeser, "Information Technology and the Future of Cities," *Journal of Urban Economics* 43, no. 1 (1998): 136–56; Storper and Venables, "Buzz."

46. Berger, *Making in America*.

47. Elisabeth B. Reynolds, "The Changing Geography of Biomanufacturing," Working Paper MIT-IPC-11-001, Cambridge, Mass.: MIT Industrial Performance Center, 2011.

48. Helper et al., *Locating American Manufacturing.*

49. Ibid.

50. Susan Helper and Howard Wial, *Accelerating Advanced Manufacturing with New Research Centers* (Washington, D.C.: Brookings Institution, 2011).

51. Ibid.

52. Sanford L. Moskowitz, *The Advanced Materials Revolution: Technology and Economic Growth in the Age of Globalization* (Hoboken, N.J.: Wiley, 2009).

53. See "Help for Businesses," NYC Small Business Services, www.nyc.gov/html/sbs/, accessed October 15, 2014.

54. Joel Rast, "The Promises and Pitfalls of Planned Manufacturing Districts: Lessons from Chicago," *Progressive Planning* 190 (Winter 2012): 21–23; D. Bradford Hunt and Jon B. DeVries, *Planning Chicago* (Chicago: American Planning Association, 2013).

55. Nathanael Z. Hoelzel and Nancey Green Leigh, "Atlanta: How to Remake Cities as Places for Twenty-First Century Manufacturing," *Progressive Planning* 190 (Winter 2012): 35–39; Rast, "Promises and Pitfalls of Planned Manufacturing Districts"; Hunt and DeVries, *Planning Chicago.*

56. Helper et al., *Why Does Manufacturing Matter?*

The Influence of Technology on Advanced Manufacturing, Private R&D, and Infrastructure

DISCUSSANT: RANDY BLANKENHORN

CHICAGO METROPOLITAN AGENCY FOR PLANNING (CMAP)

Technologies are transforming the how, what, and where of manufacturing. This is an excellent lens through which to view the globalized economy and its effects on regions like metropolitan Chicago. This "manufacturing moment" could reverse the trends of job losses and outsourcing and take advantage of the opportunities afforded by a new wave of advanced manufacturing. Our regional manufacturing cluster produces two-thirds of metropolitan Chicago's exports, provides wages 27 percent higher than the regional average, fuels 85 percent of the region's private research and development, and influences nearly every major industry.[1]

As manufacturers become more concerned about supply chains, intellectual property protections, and increasing overseas costs of labor and energy, the United States must embrace high-tech advanced manufacturing that plays to our nation's strengths. We need to

- focus on products that are complex, innovative, and difficult to replicate,
- find new process efficiencies that will make manufacturing more productive,
- create a workforce that has the specialized skills to maximize the commercial impacts of these products and processes, and
- capitalize on the transportation infrastructure that is our global economic advantage, particularly in the Chicago region.

But how does this opportunity influence the growth and development of urban areas? As Dr. Howard Wial of the University of Illinois at Chicago stated in his paper for the 2013 session of the UIC Urban Forum, "New manufacturing technologies do not exist in a spatial vacuum. American manufacturing is overwhelmingly located in metropolitan areas, and high-technology manufacturing even more so."[2] Dr. Wial demonstrates the clear advantages of manufacturing located in metropolitan areas with both the density of talent to design and develop goods and the ability to easily access consumers. Advanced manufacturing firms will cluster where there is significant access to skilled labor, efficient supply chains for both international trade and local suppliers, and a seamless transition from research and design to the factory floor. To support the development of advanced manufacturing, metropolitan regions must "draw on the same competitive advantages that fueled growth a century ago—economic innovation, infrastructure assets, and a deep pool of skilled workers."[3]

FOSTERING INNOVATION

As the home to world-class universities—and as the only region with two national laboratories—metropolitan Chicago has extensive assets for public research and development. But we need to do more to realize our potential, and the region has recently experienced a severe decline in private R&D employment and output. Between 1980 and 2000, metropolitan Chicago's private R&D output tripled, and it was ranked consistently as the nation's second-largest research center. For example, in 2000 the region's R&D output was 40 percent larger than Boston's, but just ten years later, Boston's output doubled that of the Chicago region.[4] Another source of concern is that 85 percent of private R&D spending in metropolitan Chicago is by firms with five hundred or more employees, while almost 84 percent of the region's manufacturing firms employ fewer than fifty workers. According to Scott Miller, interim director of the Illinois Manufacturing Lab, "there is a significant research gap for small and medium-sized manufacturers"[5] who are becoming increasingly responsible for the technological changes demanded by those companies further up the manufacturing chain. Howard Wial agrees, and challenges research institutions to develop a system for "small- and medium-sized firms who have research problems that aren't getting worked on."[6]

For metropolitan Chicago and the rest of the nation, it is imperative that we increase funding for public and private investment in research. But research alone isn't enough. We need to do a much better job of getting from idea to product to market. As Scott Miller says, "We don't do a good job of commercializing our research. We have great ideas here, and someone else takes it and commercializes—getting the fruits of our labor."[7] We must connect technology to manufacturers, particularly those that are small and medium-sized businesses, in a way that creates new markets and takes advantage of existing ones. Effective partnerships between academia, government, and the private sector must be developed to take advantage of the technological innovation that is creating new products, processes, and markets.

INFRASTRUCTURE ADVANTAGE

The size and strength of the freight cluster in metropolitan areas, particularly in metropolitan Chicago, make them well-positioned to take advantage the current manufacturing moment. The region's ability to move raw materials and finished products efficiently is essential to competitiveness in a global economy. Metropolitan regions offer options for moving freight by truck, rail, water, and air, "enabling firms to tailor freight moves to specific firm needs."[8] But metropolitan areas retain that transportation advantage only as long as those systems remain efficient. According to Howard Wial, "mechanization means labor costs are less of a factor in competitiveness,"[9] making reduced transportation costs even more important in the location decisions for manufacturing.

Metropolitan regions offer accessibility to both suppliers and markets. Today's advanced manufacturing processes entail many steps, from supplying raw materials to the manufacturing of parts and components to assembling finished products. "Even in today's globalized economy, most manufacturing flows still are regional: Half of all manufactured goods in the U.S. move less than 50 miles, underscoring the importance of regional supply chains."[10] However, pervasive congestion in regions such as ours significantly reduces reliability, negating some of our transportation advantages.

Innovations in supply chain logistics allow for lower costs, improve access to global, national, and regional markets, and control inventory flows. Among the fastest-growing segments of our region's economy, logistics firms are providing innovative solutions that focus on improving the reliability of goods movement. These firms thrive in regions that have concentrated goods movements with multimodal options and complex supply chains. Metropolitan regions currently provide accessibility for logistics firms with access to freight suppliers who rely on efficient transportation systems. The logistics sector exemplifies how technology can be used to transform how manufacturers access supplies and markets.

However, without significant investment in our nation's and region's transportation infrastructure, this natural advantage of metropolitan areas is severely compromised. On roads and rails and at airports, traffic congestion increases transportation costs in both time and money, discouraging manufacturers from investing in our urban areas. Although major investment in transportation is necessary to retain our competitive advantage, metropolitan areas are unable to simply add more capacity to our systems to solve the problems. We need to better manage the system by separating freight and passenger traffic wherever possible, both on our highways and our rails.

To manage traffic flow, we need to implement "congestion pricing," which gives drivers the option of using an express toll lane that ensures reliable travel times. Supply chain and logistics managers can deal with longer travel times as long as those times are reliable. Express toll lanes give users of the transportation system additional choices that can be used to meet important schedules, both for passenger traffic and freight traffic.

WORKFORCE MATTERS

Access to skilled workers is as important to manufacturers as the efficient delivery of goods. The ability to develop advanced manufacturing facilities on smaller parcels in denser, mixed-use areas allows for a larger pool of skilled workers closer to the plant site. But improved public transit service that gives employees increased options about where to live is a key to attracting young, skilled workers who increasingly wish to live in more urban areas.

Today's advanced manufacturing workforce has changed significantly from its historical roots, relying on more critical thinking and technological aptitude. As the manufacturing economy continues to grow, these businesses face increasing shortages in the skilled labor required to capitalize on this opportunity. A wave of retirements by older workers who have transformed their skills to meet the needs of advanced manufacturing will leave significant worker shortages over the next decade. Our educational system has not filled the gap in providing the necessary training to produce the next wave of employees who will meet the needs of today's and tomorrow's manufacturing. According to Herman Brewer, bureau chief of economic development for Cook County, "We have gotten away from vocational training in high schools and have been unable to meet the needs for a very specific skill set."[11] Howard Wial agrees: "We do a terrible job of providing the right kind of educational training and certificates for people who don't need a college degree."[12]

Improving the quality of science, technology, engineering, and math (STEM) curricula in our grade schools and high schools will give manufacturing workers the baseline skills necessary to be successful in advanced manufacturing. Training services need to be better coordinated, with "stackable credentials" that not only give workers a career path, but also provide employers confidence that workers have acquired the necessary skills. These programs must be flexible to meet employers' needs. According to Scott Miller, "Changing curriculum to meet businesses needs takes too long."[13] Educational institutions, training providers, and employers must commit to improving the process to provide flexible, simple, coordinated processes for real-time workforce training that better meets the needs of business and workers.

CONCLUSION

Emerging technologies have the potential to thrive in metropolitan regions that provide the skilled workers, transportation infrastructure, innovation, and commercialization necessary to take advantage of this manufacturing moment. The resulting growth can change how our urban areas develop, taking advantage of their unique assets. But unless we invest in those assets to make advanced manufacturing attractive in metropolitan areas, this moment will pass us by.

Notes

1. Chicago Metropolitan Agency for Planning (CMAP), "Metropolitan Chicago's Manufacturing Cluster: A Drill-Down Report on Innovation Workforce and Infrastructure," last modified February 2013, accessed October 16 2014, www.cmap .illinois.gov.

2. Howard Wial, "A Factory in Every Home? Emerging Manufacturing Technologies and Metropolitan Development," paper presented at the UIC Urban Forum, Chicago, Illinois, December 5, 2013. See also Wial's chapter of the same title in this book.

3. CMAP, "Metropolitan Chicago's Manufacturing Cluster."

4. Illinois Innovation Network, Illinois Innovation Index, accessed October 16 2014, www.illinoisinnovation.com; CMAP, "Metropolitan Chicago's Manufacturing Cluster."

5. Scott Miller, interim director, Illinois Manufacturing Lab, at UIC Urban Forum, December 5, 2013.

6. Wial, "Factory in Every Home?"

7. Miller, at UIC Urban Forum.

8. Chicago Metropolitan Agency for Planning (CMAP), "The Freight-Manufacturing Nexus: Metropolitan Chicago's Built-in Advantage," last modified August 2013, accessed October 16 2014, www.cmap.illinois.gov.

9. Wial, "Factory in Every Home?"

10. CMAP, "Freight-Manufacturing Nexus."

11. Herman Brewer, bureau chief, Cook County Bureau of Economic Development, at UIC Urban Forum, December 5, 2013.

12. Wial, "Factory in Every Home?"

13. Miller, at UIC Urban Forum.

Workforce Development and Technology

DARRELL M. WEST

BROOKINGS INSTITUTION

EXECUTIVE SUMMARY

Workforce development in the science, technology, engineering, and math (STEM) area is of tremendous importance in the United States. It is vital for economic growth and long-term prosperity. A study found that "STEM occupations are projected to grow by 17.0 percent from 2008 to 2018, compared to 9.8 percent growth for non-STEM occupations."[1]

By 2018, the United States is going to have 8 million STEM jobs, or 4.9 percent of all the jobs in the U.S. economy.[2] At that time, we will need 2.4 million new STEM workers in the areas of computers (1.2 million), engineering (676,000), life and physical sciences (302,000), architecture (143,000), and math (49,000). Of these jobs, 37 percent will occur in professional and business services, 19 percent in manufacturing, 13 percent in government and public education, 9 percent in finance, and the remainder in natural resources and mining, private education, wholesale/retail trade, transportation, and health care services, among other fields.[3]

Overall, according to the U.S. Bureau of Labor Statistics, the information sector will rise from around $1.2 to $1.9 trillion between 2010 and 2020 and become the fastest-growing segment in the U.S. economy. Much of the increase is expected to come from "software publishers and the data processing, hosting, related services, and other information services industries."[4]

Similar increases are projected in other areas, such as health care and education, where technology is changing the nature of job requirements. In the health care area, for example, planners anticipate new jobs in health information technology, data management, data analytics, informatics, and information sciences.[5] As pointed out by Forouzan Golshani and colleagues, "the concept of information is no longer specific to certain domains of academic endeavor (such as computer science, management information, etc.) but is instead becoming an integral part of the everyday activity of human life."[6]

Yet despite the growing demand for workers, we lack sufficient numbers and training of employees in science fields. Many U.S. students are not seeking degrees in STEM areas. And of those who do, a number drop out and fail to complete their programs. The result is that employers in many places report difficulty filling available technology positions. At the same time, the United States is facing a major retirement wave as baby boomers leave the workforce in coming years. By 2020, according to the U.S. Bureau of Labor Statistics, one-quarter of workers will be fifty-five years or older.[7]

This paper looks at workforce development challenges in the science and technology areas. What is the extent of skill shortages in the U.S. economy? Why aren't women and minorities entering the STEM workforce in numbers proportional to their presence in the overall population? How does the distribution of STEM jobs vary across cities and neighborhoods? How effective are educational initiatives and retraining programs at preparing people for the workforce of tomorrow?

In this analysis, I argue that cities and states need to undertake decisive action designed to address STEM workforce issues. In particular, I suggest the following:

1. There are serious issues related to the few students graduating with STEM degrees, problems of underrepresentation among women and minority students, and difficulty hiring technology workers among certain sectors.

2. There is tremendous variation across cities and neighborhoods in job distribution and skill sets, and these differences affect economic development.

3. Many workforce development programs are fragmented, not well-funded, and have widely varying effectiveness depending on structure, operations, and the organizer.

4. To fill current gaps and boost long-term development, it is important that cities and states add programs that attract more STEM students, strengthen community colleges, turn STEM into STEAM (science, technology, engineering, arts, and math), improve transparency in workforce training programs, integrate existing pro-

grams, launch online training programs, expand apprenticeship programs, develop magnet schools, and help the national government reform immigration.

THE EXTENT OF SKILL SHORTAGES

There are a number of problems in the workforce area that affect cities and states. The United States has too few students studying STEM fields, and there is underrepresentation of women and minorities. A number of companies in various metropolitan areas report difficulty in hiring technology workers. Current immigration policies prevent foreign students with STEM degrees from staying in the United States and meeting workforce needs through that route.

Too Few STEM Graduates to Satisfy Workforce Needs

A number of researchers have found that insufficient numbers of U.S.-born young people are receiving training in science and engineering fields to satisfy workforce needs. A report from the Economic Policy Institute, for example, found that "while there were strong increases in the number of computer science graduates and entrants from other fields that supply the IT industry during the late 1990s, after the dot-com bubble burst in 2001 a declining number of both guestworkers and U.S. students entered the IT pipeline." Since that time period, there have been too few U.S.-born workers in the information technology (IT) area to meet workforce needs.[8]

That analysis found that "only 4 percent of high school graduates go on to earn a STEM degree in college, and the share that actually takes a STEM job one year after graduation is even lower, just 2.5 percent."[9] According to the institute, part of the reason is that the large supply of guestworkers has kept wages down, and therefore income levels have not acted as a sufficient incentive for young people to enter that field.

Another report pointed out that "candidates for training programs for manufacturing technicians often lack the math skills necessary to succeed in these rigorous programs." Author Dan Fogarty has noted that "an insufficient skill in applied math is the most commonly cited barrier both for incumbent workers and candidates for hire."[10]

Many high school students in the United States report little interest or proficiency in science and mathematics. An ACT study found that "fewer than one in five 12th graders have both high interest in STEM and high proficiency in mathematics—precursors to success in STEM undergraduate programs."[11]

Of the 1.7 million college freshmen, only 233,000 are expected to graduate with STEM degrees. This number is well below the 2.4 million new technology jobs that will be required for our twenty-first-century economy.

Emerging fields such as nanotechnology, genetics, and bioengineering require knowledge of science, math, and engineering. Yet it is hard to find people with the appropriate training in this area. As noted by Stephen Fonash, "the U.S. education system is not geared, for the most part, to teaching a unified approach to understanding and using science and engineering."[12] This lack of integration means that some of those new STEM graduates will not have all the skills needed for the expected positions.

One of the striking findings of an analysis of American Community Survey data is that "the vast majority of workers who have been trained in science and engineering are not currently working in a STEM occupation." Researcher Liana Christin Landivar found that only 26 percent of those who graduate with a degree in science and engineering have jobs in those areas. Many of them are employed instead in fields such as "health care, law, education, social work, accounting, or counseling."[13]

These issues are particularly problematic for cities and states given the coming retirement wave of baby boomers. That is a development that will exacerbate current shortages in the IT field. For example, a survey of chief information officers found that "a quarter of state CIOs predict that between 21 and 30 percent of state IT employees will be eligible for retirement within the next five years." This ticking time bomb makes it all the more imperative that we recruit young people into science and technology.

Problems Facing Women and Minority Students

Women and minority students face particular challenges in the STEM area. They are underrepresented in these fields and face particular obstacles in pursuing science and technology courses of study. According to research undertaken by the U.S. Department of Commerce, "women are vastly underrepresented in STEM jobs and among STEM degree holders despite making up nearly half of the U.S. workforce."[14] Right now, they occupy only 24 percent of STEM positions, compared to 48 percent for the overall economy.

The same report identifies several possible reasons for this underrepresentation. Its authors note that "STEM career paths may be less accommodating to people cycling in and out of the workforce to raise a family—or it may be because there are relatively few female STEM role models. Perhaps strong gender stereotypes discourage women from pursuing STEM education and STEM jobs."[15]

In addition, studies have found that women face barriers in terms of the quality of educational experiences. For example, they aren't always encouraged to take STEM courses, and they aren't steered into STEM internships or summer positions. This limits their exposure to science opportunities and makes it difficult for them to advance professionally in these fields.

An analysis of longitudinal data concludes that "the structure of majors and their linkages to professional training and careers may combine with gender differences in educational goals to influence the persisting gender gap in STEM fields."[16] Sociologists Allison Mann and Thomas DiPrete argue that the problem is not gender differences in math scores but the manner in which fields such as math and chemistry are structured. There is a "gendering of the pathways from major to occupation" that filters out women.

There are similar challenges in regard to the entry of minority students into science and math fields. In 2011, only 6 percent of the STEM workforce were African American, about half of their percentage in the overall population. Hispanics also are underrepresented in STEM and constitute only around 7 percent of the labor force.[17]

For both female and minority students, there are outright biases that discourage entry into science programs. One randomized double-blind study found that when asked to rate the application materials for a lab manager position, science faculty were more likely to rate "the male applicant as significantly more competent and hirable than the (identical) female applicant. These participants also selected a higher starting salary and offered more career mentoring to the male applicant."[18] That obviously weakens women's training opportunities and creates barriers to their long-term advancement.

When one looks at the percentage of women enrolled in science and engineering graduate programs, though, there are some promising signs. According to National Science Foundation data, "nearly half of the 611,600 S&E graduate students enrolled in the United States in fall 2009 were women." However, a number of these women do not complete doctoral degrees. The report found that "women earned 41% of S&E doctoral degrees awarded in the United States in 2008."[19]

And when one analyzes early access to STEM subjects, girls (30 percent) enrolled in Algebra I during junior high school outnumber the boys (27 percent). Girls also are passing these courses by a slightly higher amount. Eighty-five percent of girls pass these classes in grades 7 or 8 compared to 83 percent of boys.[20]

Statistics demonstrate that few minority students are focusing on STEM at the graduate levels. Of the pupils pursuing doctorates in STEM areas, only very few come from minority backgrounds. The limited size of this pool poses enormous challenges to increasing the number of minority students graduating with STEM expertise.

The Impact of Restrictive Immigration Rules

Surveys estimate that about one-quarter of the STEM workforce having college degrees are immigrants. They have found employers willing to sponsor visas for them, and they have navigated the complexities of current policies.[21]

But researchers also have found that three-quarters of foreign graduates of U.S. universities with degrees in a STEM discipline would like to stay in the United States. They enjoy the professional opportunities that exist in this country and the chance to earn a good standard of living compared to their home countries. They face obstacles, though, that prevent them from remaining here.[22] They have the skills required to fill the job vacancies noted above, but can't secure visas.[23]

For example, the H-1B visa program focuses on highly skilled workers, for whom it makes available 65,000 visas each year, plus some additional numbers not counted under the cap.[24] In many years, however, these visas are gone in a short period of time. In 2007, the full number had been issued by the end of the first month of the year.[25] In 2008, there were 163,000 applicants for the 65,000 available slots.[26] Even in the recessionary years of 2009 and 2010, these visas were taken before the end of each year.[27] This leaves many individuals unable to get an entry visa although they have job offers in the United States. And if they do get a visa, it is restricted to employment with particular companies, which in some cases limits worker mobility and promotions.

The situation with temporary H-1B visas is problematic because of the inability to bring on needed workers in short supply. "When the cap hits, we are not able to on-board until there is a new supply of visas," said Robin Paulino, Microsoft's senior attorney for global migration in an interview. "Sometimes, there is a four- to five-month wait."[28]

Google generally has found that around one-third of its H-1B visa applications have been denied, which constrained hiring and job creation. In 2008, it submitted three hundred H-1B visa applications, but ninety were not approved. U.S. citizens or permanent residents comprise 90 percent of its workforce, so it needs to fill the remaining 10 percent of its staffing needs with immigrants.[29]

The difficulties of the visa process force companies into targeting applications on high-level individuals. Rob Russell of Life Technologies said: "We don't sponsor visas for someone who is a junior-level financial analyst. That would never get through immigration long-term. We are now sponsoring one-third of the workforce outside the U.S. We focus on specialty positions where we can get visas."[30]

A number of high-tech companies report difficulties of worker shortages and missed opportunities arising from current immigration policies. Officials at Microsoft, Google, Intel, Cisco, and Hewlett-Packard complain that they cannot hire all the engineers and computer scientists they need.[31]

Brad Smith, the General Counsel for Microsoft, testified before Congress that "filling our talent needs remains a serious challenge. For example, in May [2011], Microsoft had 4,551 unfilled job openings, of which 2,629 were for computer science positions. In 2011, it has taken us on average 65 days to fill openings for experienced candidates in core tech positions in the United States."[32]

Jack Chen, an immigration attorney for Microsoft, explained to me that there is "a very competitive labor market for the right talent." Some technology fields have unemployment rates of 3 to 4 percent, he noted. "For every available and talented worker with the right skills, there are multiple job opportunities."[33]

Christine Scullion, the director of human resources for the National Association of Manufacturing, said "manufacturing is not what it used to be. It requires advanced skills that many folks don't have. We focus a lot on skill-building even in entry level manufacturing jobs. We work to build the domestic pipeline for entry level jobs. We have to focus on STEM education and getting Americans to go into STEM fields. . . . I talked to someone the other day who said there are 1,700 PhD graduates focusing on technology, but there are 3,000 open jobs. We don't have enough workers in the domestic pipeline."[34]

Half of the state governments (54.8 percent) report "difficulty recruiting new employees to fill vacant IT positions." Among the specific areas where state officials report the great difficulty finding employees are security (52.4 percent of states report difficulty), project management (50 percent), application development (47.6 percent), virtual architecture (47.6 percent), analysis and design (42.9 percent), and networking support (40.5 percent).[35]

The result of the visa cap is that many highly trained foreign students with expertise in STEM fields return to their native countries. Even though the United States has trained and educated these individuals, they end up going home and building businesses that otherwise would have been located in U.S. cities and states. This limits the size and quality of the STEM workforce in the United States.

VARIATION ACROSS U.S. CITIES AND NEIGHBORHOODS

There are serious problems of technology worker recruitment and training at the national level, but the trends cited mask large differences across cities and neighborhoods. Not every region and locale experiences these problems at the same level or in the same way. Some are more successful than others at building a well-trained workforce than others.

In *Place Matters*, urban specialists Peter Dreier, John Mollenkopf, and Todd Swanstrom argue that geography has tremendous consequences for education, housing, crime, health, transportation, and job creation. "Economic segregation reinforces income inequality, which then fuels economic segregation," they note.[36] Due to their generally more centralized approach to school funding and family assistance, European countries have fewer problems related to geography than the United States.

In recent decades, for example, "job sprawl" has drawn employment opportunities away from downtown metropolitan areas. With wealth residing outside central cities and in the suburbs, it was not surprising that many businesses have followed people and we have seen the suburbanization of jobs.

Between 1998 and 2006, jobs in nearly every sector (including science and technology) moved away from downtowns to the suburbs. Job growth increased by 1.2 percent in areas more than ten miles from the downtown, while they decreased 10.4 percent for areas less than three miles from the downtown and by 5.4 percent for areas three to ten miles away from the downtown. According to a Brookings Metropolitan Policy program study, "by 2010 nearly twice the share of jobs was located at least 10 miles away from downtown (43 percent) as within three miles of downtown (23 percent)."[37]

The geographic diversification of employment patterns has had profound consequences for worker training and educational development. As jobs shifted to the suburbs, there have been pressures on training programs to expand so that they could be close to workers and provide them with the necessary skills. Colleges in a number of areas have opened suburban branches, and workforce development activities have spread around the region.

Of course, repositioning workforce programs has not necessarily helped displaced workers located in the urban core. When their jobs moved, many of them did not have the mobility to follow employers. These workers were trapped in areas with few jobs, poor transportation options other than cars, and a declining number of retraining programs to assist their work transition. This perpetuated a spatial mismatch between employers and the unemployed, and made it difficult for the displaced to upgrade their work skills.

This has led some scholars such as Pauline Lipman to call for a "new political economy." She says that race, education, and urban development are interconnected and that we need a social justice perspective to our thinking about community development. According to her, we shouldn't rely solely on the marketplace to move cities but should have a more expansive view of metropolitan life.[38]

Inequity was particularly accentuated during the Great Recession of 2009 and thereafter, when more than nine million people lost jobs and unemployment reached double-digit levels. The broad scope of that downturn and the stress it placed on worker training programs was challenging for many sectors and contributed to the human suffering of that downturn.

When one looks at the hundred largest metropolitan areas, there are substantial variations in where jobs are found. The cities that exhibited the largest increase in jobs located more than ten miles from the downtown area included Cape Coral–Fort Myers, Florida (with increases of 3 percent); Little Rock, Arkansas (1.8 percent); San Antonio, Texas (1.7 percent); Provo, Utah (1.7 percent); El Paso, Texas (1.6 percent); Phoenix, Arizona (1.5 percent); Oklahoma City, Oklahoma (1.5 percent); Charlotte, North Carolina (1.5 percent); Honolulu, Hawaii (1.3 percent); and Birmingham, Alabama (1.3 percent).[39]

Meanwhile, the locales showing the largest increase in jobs found within three miles of the downtown included Chattanooga, Tennessee (an increase of 2.5 percent); New Orleans, Louisiana (1.8 percent); Louisville, Kentucky (1.8 percent); Charleston, South Carolina (1.7 percent); Cincinnati, Ohio (1.6 percent); Chicago, Illinois (1.6 percent); San Jose, California (1.5 percent); Milwaukee, Wisconsin (1.5 percent); Seattle, Washington (1.3 percent); and Austin, Texas (1.3 percent).[40]

In addition to where jobs are found, metropolitan areas vary enormously in the size of their STEM workforce. Using data from the U.S. Department of Labor's Employment and Training Administration, researchers have found that 20 percent of U.S. jobs (26 million in total) require at least one aspect of STEM knowledge. Half of these are not in traditional information technology areas but reside in sectors such as manufacturing, health care, and construction, which have a technology component.[41]

Of the hundred largest metropolitan areas, those cities having the highest proportion of STEM jobs include San Jose, California (33 percent of all jobs); Washington, D.C. (27 percent); Palm Beach, Florida (27 percent); Seattle, Washington (26 percent); Madison, Wisconsin (24 percent); Boston, Massachusetts (24 percent); Houston, Texas (23 percent); Baltimore, Maryland (23 percent); and San Diego, California (23 percent).[42]

Those with the lowest include McAllen, Texas (11 percent); Modesto, California (13 percent); Las Vegas, Nevada (13 percent); Stockton, California (14 percent); Lakeland, Florida (15 percent); Scranton, Pennsylvania (16 percent); Youngstown, Ohio (16 percent); and Lancaster, Pennsylvania (16 percent).[43]

These contrasts show that not all places devote the same effort to or generate similar success when it comes to STEM job creation. Some areas have made tremendous progress on this dimension while others are struggling with economies still trapped in an industrial-era mentality.

The lack of attention to local STEM economies is problematic because there is a strong link between STEM employment and overall metropolitan innovation, economic competitiveness, and financial well-being. According to the Brookings Metropolitan Policy program, "greater STEM skills at the metro level are strongly associated with higher patents per worker (an indicator of innovation), lower unemployment, a lower rate of job losses during the recent recession and early recovery, higher exports as a share of gross domestic product (GDP) (a measure of international competitiveness), and higher incomes."[44] Without more attention to worker skills in the STEM area, some cities will face a difficult economic future.

FRAGMENTATION OF WORKFORCE DEVELOPMENT AND DECLINES IN FEDERAL FUNDING

In 1998, Congress passed the Workforce Investment Act (WIA) with an eye toward improving labor training. It replaced the Job Training Partnership Act and set the goals of providing greater flexibility at the local level and enabling community-based organizations to become more innovative in their retraining programs. The bill did this through the development of Workforce Investment Boards chaired by a business representative. At least half of the board was mandated to come from the business community in order to ensure a strong community connection.

Yet analysts have found that the legislation has not fundamentally improved the situation for many cities and states. According to University of California professor Karen Chapple, WIA "has created an inefficient and fragmented employment and training system that fails the neediest and creates a highly differentiated landscape of opportunity across and within regions."[45] The focus on local flexibility exacerbated coordination problems and generated a patchwork of programs that varied enormously in performance and effectiveness. A number of programs remain unconnected to local employers and do not teach the kinds of skills needed in the marketplace.

A study of Workforce Investment Boards in California found there was little coordination or communication across the community boards. A number of them had only automated phone numbers, which meant that recipients had to physically visit the office in order to procure relevant information.[46] In this situation, it was hard for those requiring assistance to get help. And it was difficult for one board to learn from the experiences of other boards in the area.

A review of the federally funded Trade Adjustment Assistance (TAA) program designed for dislocated workers found considerable frustration with training activities. Interviews with program participants revealed "a general dissatisfaction with the processes, services and programs, and outcomes associated with TAA. Survey and focus group results indicate these workers found TAA services and processes cumbersome and time-consuming and actually had the effect of discouraging their education, training, and self-employment."[47]

These problems have been exacerbated because federal funding has declined precipitously over the past few decades. Economist Harry Holzer has reviewed workforce development programs and finds that "we spend fewer and fewer public (federal) dollars on workforce development over time." With the exception of Pell grants, many training programs have witnessed "dramatic declines in funding."[48] The WIA, for example, totals around $5.5 billion in support of adult, youth, and displaced worker programs, along with the Job Corps. This represents a considerable reduction from the $17 billion spent on these kinds of activities in 1979.[49]

Speaking at a Brookings Institution Manufacturing Forum, Representative David Cicilline (D-RI) complained that federal legislation has consolidated thirty-five programs and frozen funding. "We need better coordination of what employers need and what skills are provided," he said. "It is important to have private-sector involvement in these programs. The least successful programs are run by local government. The better ones are operated by private industry."[50]

Program effectiveness varies considerably depending on the type of training. An analysis of Florida college educational programs, for example, has shown that people with four-year degrees can make as much $35,400 per year, but that those with only one or two years of career-oriented community college training may make as little as $24,100.[51]

In Washington state, though, evaluation of eleven programs found positive gains for nine of the eleven. Researchers compared those in with those not in these programs and analyzed a variety of outcome measures, such as job history, wages, hours worked per quarter, food stamp assistance, Medicaid, and Temporary Assistance for Needy Families, both on short- and long-term bases.

In general, they found that program participants had significant employment and income gains compared to those not participating in the programs. They were more likely to have jobs, earn money, and avoid various forms of public assistance. Overall, these program impacts ranged from 7 to 30 percent improvements.[52]

The strongest programs integrate training around a number of different arenas. Robert Giloth of the Annie E. Casey Foundation has written that "today's workforce development implies more than employment training in the narrow sense." Instead, there needs to be integration around several elements. This includes "employer engagement, deep community connections, career advancement, integrative human service supports, contextual and industry-driven education and training, reformed community colleges, and connective tissue of networks."[53]

The City of Chicago has generated promising results by linking workforce development to economic development agreements. When it provides tax breaks and/or infrastructure assistance to particular companies, the City works with those businesses to identify new positions, needed job skills, and local organizations who can supply the necessary employees.[54] This allows more people in the city, business, and labor pools to benefit from economic expansion activities.

RECOMMENDATIONS FOR FUTURE ACTION

This paper has identified a number of problems regarding workforce development. There are shortages of workers in the science, technology, engineering, and math areas that have harmed economic growth. These challenges have made it difficult for firms to recruit the personnel they need. They have had difficulty finding either U.S.-born workers or people from other countries with the required skills and training.

Of course, cities vary widely in how acute these problems are. In general, U.S. educational institutions and workforce development programs have not been effective in addressing these problems in a number of places. Current programs are fragmented and poorly aligned to employer needs, and there have been serious cutbacks in federal support for retraining workers. This had made it difficult for workers displaced in certain industries to find jobs in the technology sector.

Cities and states need to do more to attract students into STEM fields, strengthen community colleges, turn STEM into science, technology, engineering, arts, and math (STEAM), improve transparency in workforce training programs, provide stronger integration of development activities, launch online training programs, expand apprenticeship programs, develop STEM magnet schools, and encourage the national government to reform immigration.

Doing More to Attract STEM Students— Including Women and Minorities

There are several different ways to attract more students into the science and technology (S&T) areas. K–12 schools as well as colleges and universities should set up mentoring programs that offer career advice to those interested in S&T. Student advisors need to understand that many fields outside of traditional math and computer science areas involve information technology.

For example, there are a growing number of health care and education positions that require knowledge of computers, data management, and data analytics, among other skill sets. Students need to understand that these are rapidly growing sectors and employers are looking for people who can bridge the gap between information delivery systems and substantive knowledge.

These kinds of programs are especially valuable for women and minorities, who sometimes face special challenges due to the absence of role models in science fields, not to mention subtle but significant barriers to entry into those areas. Having experts with whom they can discuss these and other challenges and people who can provide realistic advice will help improve the diversity of STEM disciplines.

Another valuable way for students to learn about science fields is through laboratory assignments and internships. Making sure that high schools, community colleges, and universities offer these types of experiences is important for the future technology pipeline. If we can make sure people have early opportunities to learn these subjects, it will increase the odds of individuals having the kinds of skills for which employers are looking.

It is crucial that K–12 STEM teachers have appropriate career incentives and professional development opportunities. Some schools provide extra monetary supplements for those with experience in the area. Relevant teachers are given regular chances to upgrade their knowledge and to hear from experts in fields that change rapidly. Unless students experience quality teaching in science classrooms, it will be hard to keep them on the track to more advanced skills in these areas.

As part of its Educate to Innovate campaign, the Obama administration has provided over $700 million to train ten thousand new science and math teachers. This includes financial assistance and training partnerships. A notable example is an agreement between the National Aeronautics and Space Administration and the Girl Scouts of the USA to encourage young women to pursue science training. As part of this partnership, NASA officials spoke at the 2012 Girl Scout annual convention and demonstrated hands-on STEM activities that would encourage girls to go into science.[55]

The National Science Foundation funded a Tri-Regional Information Technology project that provided after-school technology training for high school girls in northern Florida. Participants were given 280 hours of IT instruction over two years. A comparison of pre- and post-questionnaire responses found that the program increased girls' knowledge about and confidence in technology.[56] This suggests the value of training programs aimed at underrepresented populations.

Strengthening Community Colleges

Along with four-year institutions, community colleges play a vital role in worker training. The 1,045 community colleges across the United States educate 6.2 million students each year. This is about 35 percent of all the college and university students in the nation.[57]

Their role in workforce development is especially important in many metropolitan areas. For students from disadvantaged backgrounds, community colleges sometimes are the educator of last resort. Extending the lifeline that is needed for these individuals, they equip students with concrete and practical skills.

These institutions fulfill these roles because of their ease of entry, which is one of their strengths. Students can enroll at a relatively inexpensive price. Community colleges have flexible programs and hours for students to take courses. In addition, people find that their course offerings are concrete and practical.

Community colleges are helpful for workforce development because they hire instructors from industry and thereby help to connect graduates to local companies. These individuals serve as valuable intermediaries who bridge demand and supply in the workforce. They also help build "career ladders" that provide a structured job placement service for trained students.

Yet despite the importance of community colleges for workforce development, only about 20 percent of federal STEM funding supports education at two-year institutions.[58] Most of federal financing is aimed at four-year colleges and universities, in the form of financial aid and R&D grants from the National Science Foundation, National Institutes of Health, and the Department of Defense.

Although they provide good access, community colleges need to do a better job meeting their educational mission. More than half of the students enrolled in community colleges fail to earn a two-year degree or to transfer to a four-year school.[59] Their high attrition rates undermine the role they could play in advancing workforce development. By strengthening their educational programs, we could expand the opportunities available to a broad range of students.

States such as Oregon and Washington have done an excellent job integrating community college curricula with local workforce development programs. Government officials and business leaders work closely with educators to integrate training with their job needs. They have achieved positive results with these efforts, and their students graduate at higher levels than elsewhere. Many of them have been able to find jobs and earn a decent living following completion of these programs.

Turning STEM into STEAM

Apple cofounder Steve Jobs was famous for integrating innovative design into advanced technology products. With items such as the iPhone and iPad, he built a business and consumer product line that people loved and purchased in large numbers. His company was long considered a model for outstanding product design.

His success has inspired others to suggest that we need educational programs focused on STEAM. We need to bring together people interested in arts and design with scientists and engineers who know how to make things. That would allow those with different perspectives to learn from one another and to generate products that are practical and easy to use.

Combining art and design improves technology innovation and adds an important element of integrative thinking. Many companies have failed to grasp the close connection of these features and therefore missed the chance to get the most from their new technologies. Some of the most successful innovations have placed a high priority on art and design, and this has helped those business firms achieve impressive results in the process.

Improving Transparency in Workforce Retraining Programs

Not all programs are created alike. There clearly are major differences in the quality and results of workforce training programs. Some do a much better job of preparing their participants for businesses than others. It is thought that those that are closely connected with local businesses and that teach skills that are valued by those establishments are the ones most likely to be successful.

But a problem with retraining programs in many cities is the lack of consumer information on their effectiveness. Workers often have to decide on their enrollment without any data on completion rates, job placement results, local demands for workers, or instructor background. There clearly are important criteria for program assessment, yet if people have no access to that data, it is difficult to promote successful programs and warn applicants about those activities that are not very effective.

One innovative proposal for improving retraining program transparency is from Louis Jacobson of New Horizons Economic Research and Robert LaLonde of the University of Chicago.[60] In a paper written for the Brookings Hamilton Project, they argue that cities and states need to use data to rate the performance of retraining programs and then make that information available online. This would enable workers to see which programs were most effective.

The resulting transparency would allow the marketplace to encourage those who are doing a good job to attract more participants. This is a way to inform consumers about the quality of educational programs and use the resulting feedback loop to improve the instructional marketplace in general.

In addition, we need to pay more attention to the metrics of evaluation. It used to be that program success was defined by the ninety-day window following completion of the program. This was considered the best barometer for instructional impact.

However, advocates now argue that it is important to track performance over no less than six to twelve months. This allows evaluators to see the longer work history and whether gains are short- or longer-term in nature.[61] Having transparent data for longer periods of time would enable workers to become more discerning consumers.

Better Coordination across Training Programs

In her assessment of federal workforce development policies, Brookings Institution fellow Elisabeth Jacobs notes that there is little coordination across training programs and little integration between the public and private sectors. Programs are siloed and not very good at supplying the skills needed in the twenty-first-century job market.[62]

Having "one-stop career centers" is a way to integrate various activities and make it easier for those in need of retraining to access a range of educational services in a particular area. This would help employees in need and make it easier for employers to target their outreach efforts.

State and local governments should improve their management and communications so that training programs operate more effectively. Nothing is more problematic than operating workforce development programs that do not lead to jobs. Unless these activities can match supply with demand in the labor market, these programs will not be considered very successful.

Launching Online Training Programs

New advances in distance education offer some hope for the future.[63] Workers in rural areas and from underprivileged populations often have difficulty in getting access to all the training they need. There may not be sufficient programs in their geographic areas or retraining may not offer the particular skills that they need. Indeed, one of the challenges in the worker retraining area is matching up worker demand for skills with the program supply of retraining activities.

Online training programs help overcome geographic disparities and training mismatches. Through distance learning, a worker with Internet access in Idaho can utilize training programs in Chicago to enhance his or her skills. A number of private companies have experienced significant costs savings while continuing to deliver high-quality training.[64] There is no reason why similar efficiencies cannot be achieved in the worker retraining area.

Technology helps consumers by bringing costs down and improving access to training. Instructors can use the Internet to show workers how to develop their skills and identify job opportunities. Many have set up electronic bulletin boards where people can share data on things that are most helpful to them. These and other kinds of online programs can narrow the gap between training, employment opportunities, and job performance.

Expanding Apprenticeship Programs

Not every person needs to go to college to find a satisfying position. There are individuals who require better skills, but do not have to go to college to get a job. They can do very well simply by acquiring concrete skills and putting them to use in the workplace.

For these individuals, apprenticeship programs that link them to potential employers can be quite valuable. In Arizona, for example, the Precision Manufacturing Apprenticeship program has produced effective results in terms of worker training. They take young people and match them to experienced manufacturers and provide training on various aspects of the manufacturing process.[65]

In the state of Washington, the Aerospace Joint Apprenticeship Committee trains people for jobs in that industry. They take those seeking a vocational education and teach skills that are required in the aerospace field. The Los Angeles Trade-Tech Community College offers an apprenticeship program in various technology areas. The Grand Rapids Community College has a similar program focused on business, manufacturing, and technology.[66]

It is not just community colleges that have launched these types of apprenticeships. A number of educational programs focus on high school students, as well.[67] They include the Wisconsin Youth Apprenticeship, Raymond/Broome-Tioga Board of Cooperative Educational Services, the Maine Apprenticeship Program, and the Tech Ready Apprentices for Careers in Kentucky (TRACK) program. Each of these matches up those seeking skills with trainers who have the relevant knowledge.

Some employers work in conjunction with young people to provide training for particular jobs. There are apprenticeship programs for welders, programmers, manufacturing, and business services that bridge the worlds of work and education. A number of these programs have produced well-trained graduates.[68] They demonstrate that training can take place in a variety of organizational settings and still generate positive results.

Expanding STEM Magnet Schools

Some communities have responded to the desire to encourage STEM training by establishing magnet schools for science and technology. These are schools with particular expertise in those areas and classes designed to spur interest in and knowledge about scientific matters. Secondary-level magnet schools have an excellent track record of their graduates enrolling in science majors at the undergraduate level.

Overall, about 2.5 million students attend magnet schools across the nation each year. Not all of these institutions focus on science and technology, but most have significant technology components. Teachers use digital technology to deliver instruction in innovative ways.[69]

Studies of these schools have found promising results in terms of student learning and interest. An analysis undertaken by the Civil Rights Project discovered that magnet schools showed "evidence of heightened academic achievement, very high levels of demand, and self-sustaining programs (i.e., the magnet school or program continued to flourish after the funding cycle ended)."[70]

Another research project found that "students who attend STEM-focused high schools outperformed their peers at similar institutions." They had higher test scores and a greater interest in science and math. In general,

STEM schools displayed more rigorous curricula and had innovative learning features such as internships and capstone projects.[71]

Encouraging Immigration Reform

In some sectors, foreign workers can help fill certain labor shortages in a way that helps companies grow and create additional jobs. In a number of different industries, U.S.-based companies have lost valuable growth opportunities due to problems in hiring high- and low-skilled employees. This has negatively affected firm location decisions and expansion plans. And in the long run, this has weakened overall economic growth.

Research has shown that immigrants are vital to long-term innovation and economic development in many locales. A 2011 study by the National Foundation for American Policy found that nearly half of U.S. startup companies were launched by immigrants. Of the top fifty firms, "23 had at least one immigrant founder . . . [and] 37 of the 50 companies employed at least one immigrant in a key management position such as chief technology officer."[72]

Having a growing population is a strong economic development strategy, and immigrants represent a way to expand our population and fill looming job shortages that are arising in a variety of high- and low-skill industries. Foreign-born workers can fill employment gaps and allow companies to grow and create jobs. Since employers have difficulty in filling current vacancies due to an outmoded immigration system, they are altering their recruitment and expansion plans. This suggests a need to change our current immigration system so that companies can fill STEM vacancies and cities and states can prosper.

Notes

I would like to thank Elizabeth Valentini and Hillary Schaub for outstanding research assistance.

1. David Langdon, George McKittrick, David Beede, Beethika Khan, and Mark Doms, "STEM: Good Jobs Now and for the Future," U.S. Department of Commerce, Economics and Statistics Administration, July 2011, 1.

2. Anthony Carnevale, Nicole Smith, and Michelle Melton, "STEM," Georgetown University Center on Education and the Workforce, 2011, 21.

3. Ibid., 22–24.

4. Richard Henderson, "Industry Employment and Output Projections to 2020," U.S. Bureau of Labor Statistics Monthly Labor Review, January 2012.

5. William Hersh, "The Health Information Technology Workforce: Estimations of Demands and a Framework for Requirements," *Applied Clinical Informatics* 1 (June 30, 2010).

6. Forouzan Golshani, Sethuraman Panchanathan, Oris Friesen, Y. C. Park, and J. J. Song, "A Comprehensive Curriculum for IT Education and Workforce Development: An Engineering Approach," *Proceedings of ACM SIGCSE Technical Symposium on Computer Science Education* (Association for Computing Machinery: New York, 2001), 238–42.

7. Elisabeth Jacobs, "Principles for Reforming Workforce Development and Human Capital Policies in the United States," Brookings Institution paper, December 2013, 2.

8. Hal Salzman, Daniel Kuehn, and Lindsay Lowell, "Guestworkers in the High-Skill U.S. Labor Market," Briefing Paper 359, Economic Policy Institute, April 24, 2013, 2.

9. Ibid., 5.

10. Dan Fogarty, "Pennsylvania Project for Advanced Manufacturing Careers," Pennsylvania Workforce Investment Board and the Pennsylvania Department of Labor and Industry, Harrisburg, January 14, 2010, 9.

11. Business-Higher Education Forum, "Increasing the Number of STEM Graduates: Insights from the U.S. STEM Education & Modeling Project," Business–Higher Education Forum, 2010, 2.

12. Stephen Fonash, "Education and Training of the Nanotechnology Workforce," *Journal of Nanoparticle Research*, 3 (2001): 80.

13. Liana Christin Landivar, "The Relationship between Science and Engineering Education and Employment in STEM Occupations," American Community Survey Reports, ACS-23, U.S. Census Bureau, September 2013, 2.

14. David Beede, Tiffany Julian, David Langdon, George McKittrick, Beethika Khan, and Mark Doms, "Women in STEM: A Gender Gap to Innovation," U.S. Department of Commerce, Economics and Statistics Administration, August 2011, 1.

15. Ibid., 8.

16. Allison Mann and Thomas DiPrete, "Trends in Gender Segregation in the Choice of Science and Engineering Majors," *Social Science Research* 42 (July 15, 2013): 1519.

17. Liana Christin Landivar, "Disparities in STEM Employment by Sex, Race, and Hispanic Origin," American Community Survey Reports, ACS-24, U.S. Census Bureau, September 2013, 2.

18. Corinne Moss-Racusin, John Dovidio, Victoria Brescoll, Mark Graham, and Jo Handelsman, "Science Faculty's Subtle Gender Biases Favor Male Students," *PNAS* 109 (October 9, 2012).

19. National Science Foundation, "Higher Education in Science and Engineering," ch. 2 of *Science and Engineering Indicators* 2012, 2–5.

20. U.S. Department of Education, Office for Civil Rights, "Gender Equity in Education," June 2012.

21. Sari Kerr and William Kerr, "Immigration and Employer Transitions for STEM Workers," *American Economic Review* 103 (2013): 193.

22. Edward Alden, "America's 'National Suicide,'" *Newsweek*, April 20, 2011.

23. Darrell M. West, *Brain Gain: Rethinking U.S. Immigration Policy* (Washington, D.C.: Brookings Institution Press, 2010).

24. Portions of this paper are drawn from Darrell M. West, "The Paradox of Worker Shortages at a Time of High National Unemployment," Brookings Institution paper, April 2013.

25. Roy Mark, "H1-B Visa Increase Nixed with Immigration Bill," *Internet News*, June 28, 2007.

26. Keith Wolfe and Pablo Chavez, "Tens of Thousands of Highly Skilled Workers Turned Away," Google Public Policy Blog, June 5, 2008.

27. Demetrios Papademetriou and Madeleie Sumption, *The Role of Immigration in Fostering Competitiveness in the United States* (Washington, D.C.: Migration Policy Institute, 2011), 11.

28. Robin Paulino, personal interview by the author, 2012.

29. Darrell M. West, "The Paradox of Worker Shortages at a Time of High National Unemployment," Brookings Institution paper, April 2013.

30. Rob Russell, personal interview by the author, 2012.

31. West, "The Paradox of Worker Shortages."

32. Brad Smith, "The Economic Imperative for Immigration Reform—High-Skilled Immigration as a Driver of Economic Growth," testimony before U.S. Senate Committee on the Judiciary, Subcommittee on Immigration, Refugees and Border Security, July 26, 2011.

33. Jack Chen, personal interview by the author, 2012.

34. Christine Scullion, personal interview by the author, 2012.

35. National Association of State Chief Information Officers, *State IT Workforce: Under Pressure*, January 2011, 3, 15.

36. Peter Dreier, John Mollenkopf, and Todd Swanstrom, *Place Matters: Metropolitics for the Twenty-First Century* (Lawrence: University Press of Kansas, 2001), 55.

37. Elizabeth Kneebone, "Job Sprawl Stalls: The Great Recession and Metropolitan Employment Location," Brookings Metropolitan Policy Program Report, April 2013, 1.

38. Pauline Lipman, *The New Political Economy of Urban Education: Neoliberalism, Race, and the Right to the City* (New York: Routledge, 2011).

39. Kneebone, "Job Sprawl Stalls," 6.

40. Ibid.

41. Jonathan Rothwell, "The Hidden STEM Economy," Brookings Metropolitan Policy Program Report, June 2013, 15.

42. Ibid.

43. Ibid.

44. Ibid.

45. Karen Chapple, *Promising Futures: Workforce Development and Upward Mobility in Information Technology*, (Berkeley: Institute of Urban and Regional Development, University of California at Berkeley, 2005), 12.

46. Antonio Sanchez, "Employment Training System in Los Angeles," in UCLA Luskin School of Public Affairs, "A Roadmap to Green Manufacturing" (Spring 2012): 124–33.

47. Marquita Walker, "Training for My Life: Lived Experiences of Dislocated Workers in an Advanced Manufacturing Training Program," *Advances in Social Work* 13, no. 2 (summer 2012): 275.

48. Harry Holzer, "Workforce Development as an Antipoverty Strategy," *IZA Discussion Paper*, October 2008, 1.

49. Ibid., 6.

50. Comments made at the John White Jr. Manufacturing Forum, Brookings Institution, July 10, 2013.

51. Louis Jacobson, "Improving Community College Outcome Measures Using Florida Longitudinal Schooling and Earnings Data," San Francisco, New Horizons Economic Research, May 16, 2011.

52. Kevin Hollenbeck and Wei-Jang Huang, "Net Impact and Benefit-Cost Estimates of the Workforce Development System in Washington State," Upjohn Institute Technical Report, 2006, iii.

53. Robert Giloth, "Learning from the Field: Economic Growth and Workforce Development in the 1990s," *Economic Development Quarterly* 14, no. 4 (2000): 340.

54. Joan Fitzgerald, "Moving the Workforce Intermediary Agenda Forward," *Economic Development Quarterly* 18, no. 3 (2004): 5–6.

55. Executive Office of the President of the United States, "Women and Girls in Science, Technology, Engineering, and Math," Washington, D.C., June 2013, accessed September 2013, www.whitehouse.gov/ostp/women.

56. LaDonna Morris, Linda Austin, and Amaya Davis, "Sparking Girls- Interest in Technology: The NSF Tri-IT Project," *National Social Science Journal* 39, no. 2 (2013): 60.

57. Harry Holzer and Demetra Nightingale, "Strong Students, Strong Workers: Models for Student Success through Workforce Development and Community College Partnerships," Center for American Progress, December 2009, 1.

58. Rothwell, "Hidden STEM Economy," 1.

59. Holzer and Nightingale, "Strong Students, Strong Workers," 5.

60. Louis Jacobson and Robert LaLonde, "Using Data to Improve the Performance of Workforce Training," Hamilton Project, April 2013.

61. Giloth, "Learning from the Field," 345.

62. Jacobs, "Principles for Reforming Workforce Development and Human Capital Policies in the United States," 2.

63. Jeff Stevens, Maurice Dawson, Danette Lance, and Thomas Prunier, "Online Workforce Development: A Model for Organizations to Develop a Diverse Workforce," paper delivered at the 28th Annual Conference on Distance Teaching and Learning, 2012.

64. Richard Dunn, "Getting into E-Learning for Workforce Training," *Plant Engineering*, 57, no. 9 (2003): 63–71.

65. Information on the Arizona Precision Manufacturing Apprenticeship Program can be found at www.azpmap.org/index.php/if-you-want-to-be-an-apprentice.

66. Examples include the Washington State Aerospace Joint Apprenticeship Committee at www.ajactraining.org, Los Angeles Trade-Tech Community College at http://college.lattc.edu, and Grand Rapids Community College at http://cms.grcc.edu.

67. Examples of programs targeting high school students include the Wisconsin Youth Apprenticeship, http://dwd.wisconsin.gov; Raymond/Broome-Tioga Board of Cooperative Educational Services, www.raymondcorp.com; the Maine Apprenticeship Program, www.maine.gov, and the Track KY program http://education.ky.gov.

68. Holzer and Nightingale, "Strong Students, Strong Workers," 15ff.

69. Genevieve Siegel-Hawley and Erica Frankenberg, "Reviving Magnet Schools: Strengthening a Successful Choice Option: A Research Brief," Civil Rights Project, February 2012, 19.

70. Ibid., 4.

71. Catherine Scott, "An Investigation of Science, Technology, Engineering and Mathematics (STEM) Focused High Schools in the U.S.," *Journal of STEM Education* 13, no. 5 (2012): 30.

72. Stuart Anderson, "Immigrant Founders and Key Personnel in America's 50 Top Venture-Funded Companies," National Foundation for American Policy, December 2011.

Helping Woman and Minorities See— and Reach—the Stars in STEM

DISCUSSANT: SANDEE KASTRUL

I.C.STARS

Women and minorities are underrepresented in science, technology, engineering, and math (STEM) careers. In my reflection prior to and after the panel on workforce development, I am struck by the tremendous opportunities that await us in STEM fields and by the juxtaposition of loss that is felt as a woman of color in my community.

Minorities and women of color face overt and covert losses as a result of pursuing STEM careers. We can look at the causes of low engagement, at the pipeline of students at the K–12 level engaging in STEM studies, and at how to maintain engagement with girls and minority students. Still, I believe we have to take a larger look, one that considers our perceptions and the environments we create, not just in STEM careers, but also in our communities, families, and in the popular media about the messaging of STEM opportunities.

For minorities and women of color, the losses associated with pursuing STEM careers revolve around social capital. There is an understanding among women and minorities that we have to make a great sacrifice before we can recoup our investment and realize the financial capital that can be acquired through a career in STEM. I define the difference between a sacrifice and an investment as follows: a sacrifice is something you are giving up or losing, and an investment is something you are giving to the future. This difference is important as an individual weighs the opportunity cost and the weight of return in terms of both sacrifice and investment.

For example, what if no one in your family has had a STEM career, and you were raised to see yourself as someone who would eventually work in the service industry? Next imagine that the pursuit of happiness means first family and finding a husband, then having the resources to be comfortable and to raise a family.

Imagine going to a family reunion and trying to explain your information technology (IT) programming job to a hundred relatives whose eyes glaze over as you describe how you write code for internal business applications, while your cousin who works at a job that is familiar and understood by the family is applauded for that job or good pension. Although all geeks have had the experience of loved ones not understanding what they do, as minorities we also face an underlying misunderstanding of or negative judgment about why we would take an IT job. Why would we alienate ourselves from our family and community? Why would we choose to work in a "white field" and, hardest of all, why would we want to be—*choose* to be—different and alone?

While some may argue that more women and minorities are finding opportunities in the corporate sector and that the barriers to employment based on race and gender are lower than they were two or three decades ago, the internalized notion that you will never find a husband or that your family will not understand your work only isolates you further as you take a leap and walk between two worlds.

The feeling of isolation, of walking between worlds, is palpable and can indeed affect the passion and planning that engages young people as they consider future careers. Again, if we are aspiring to pursue happiness, the odds that we will be celebrated by our families and have luck in love and marriage dwindle before our eyes, and at the end of the day it is very possible that we may be alone.

What we give up as minorities to walk between worlds. . . . That can be husbands with similar intellectual curiosity within our race, understanding from our families, cultural and community acceptance, and our identity as part of a collective or a community with shared experiences.

When the worlds of work, school, and home are so vastly different and we are constantly learning, adapting, code switching, fitting in, essentially trying to keep up, keep in, and keep our identity, it can be not just exhilarating but also exhausting. Taking this leap requires a change-making mentality, a high tolerance for risk, and the ability to accept and even embrace being uncomfortable.

STEM careers are often an oasis for smart people to find their tribe. We see this theme played over and over in popular media. The idea is that kids who are picked on in school for being geeky will one day have their reward when they are "writing the rules" as adults. The oppressed can be the oppressors or, more accurately, *we* will build tech systems, *we* will be the change agents, and *we* will earn the respect of participating in the knowledge workers movement in the future—and have the proverbial last laugh. This image is often white and male and a by-product of privilege.

But what if the cultural and societal expectations were instead that *all* citizens were problem solvers? What if the culture of innovation that we desperately try to cultivate was not a trajectory for the elite but a norm for *all* individuals? After all, aren't we each solving problems big and small every day of our lives?

In 1998, Leslie Beller and I founded i.c.stars (inner-city computer stars) to address the disparity of opportunity and to furthermore develop change agents in our communities by training resilient, change-driven individuals in technology, leadership, and business. I.c.stars is a workforce development organization and a social enterprise built in Chicago and serving both men and women. We find talent, train talent, and put talent to work. We develop change-driven individuals to excel in technology careers and to effect change as community leaders.

Some young adults already have what it takes to excel in technology careers *and* to play leadership roles in their communities. How do we know this? We discovered that the qualities that lead to excellence in technology services are closely linked to those associated with community leadership—these qualities have a "common DNA" that comes exclusively from overcoming adversity.

Individuals who have overcome adversity develop resiliency and the ability to solve complex problems.

Individuals whose communities are faced with adversity develop reciprocity and a passion for systems-level solutions.

I.c.stars unlocks this DNA through a four-month internship program, a one-year residency, and a one-year fellowship.

Upon completion of the program, individuals have six thousand hours of work experience, an associate's degree, and community service.

We currently have capacity for sixty people per year. Every quarter, we screen four hundred candidates to accept just fifteen individuals into our program. The program spans two years and requires a demanding sixty to seventy hours each week.

Organized as a 501(c)3 charitable organization, i.c.stars pursues earned-income business opportunities that further its mission. This social enterprise model is the key for growing the organization to serve more individuals and increase its impact. We have a 90 percent placement rate for our graduates in IT jobs, and the average earning increase is 300 percent. Seventy-five percent of our alumni are actively engaged in their communities through service, business, and policy, and 10 percent are homeowners. Thirty percent of our alumni are women, and 90 percent are considered minorities.

We are still here through all of the turbulence in the market, in technology, and in society because we work to create a space where people recognize that they are not alone. We are market driven, and while our framework for teaching project-based skills and behavior development does not change, the programming skills and business objectives change for each of our Fortune 500 clients. Still, we are still here because we work every day to develop leaders in a place where building solutions is celebrated, is normal, and is powerful. At i.c.stars, the word "geek" is the highest compliment because it means "expert." We are a place where women and minorities entering IT are welcomed home and told "we need you way more than you need us." We are a place where one too many can see stars.

Technology and the Workplace

A Focus on Educational Pathways

DISCUSSANT: ALFRED TATUM

The educational performance of America's youths is causing distress for the U.S. economy. Viral patterns of academic underperformance by youths in many of our nation's large urban cities and rural areas besieged by poverty and poor schooling are contributing to a multitiered economic system with low-skilled, low-wage earners and high-skilled, high-wage earners. Improving educational outcomes is critical for renewing economic development in the United States. A report by the National Center on Education and the Economy has noted that U.S. school systems produce students with reading and writing skills below what employers are seeking.[1] Equally problematic are students with inadequate math and science skills. Approximately 40 percent of high school graduates require some level of remediation in college. The proliferation of technology in the workplace and poor academic outcomes for many U.S. high school graduates present challenges that demand serious attention.

Currently, there is a mismatch between the skill set of U.S. workers and the growing demands in fields related to science, technology, engineering, and math (STEM), as discussed in Darrell West's paper at the UIC Urban Forum.[2] For many, this mismatch means that opportunities for economic advancement in certain fields will be foreclosed. There is a need to optimize solutions that explicitly and intentionally advocate for those with limited access to high-quality education and economic supports within their communities to grant them access to STEM jobs. A focus on the range of literacies (e.g., reading, mathematical, scientific) that exist across geographic landscapes should be fundamental to any discussion if the aim is to exponentially increase the participation of workers in the STEM disciplines, including those who are currently on the outside because of a multitude of barriers.

While several solutions have been proposed to fill the U.S. skill shortage in the STEM disciplines, advancing the literacy development of youths and adults is the most significant long-term economic development strategy that will benefit U.S. citizens. This is a more prudent pathway toward long-term economic vitality than less restrictive immigration legislation that would yield short-term gains for the U.S. economy by taking advantage of a talent pool of foreign or foreign-born workers because economic disparities and associated indignities in some of the nation's most underserved communities will persist.

The U.S. government is advancing several solutions that are worth noting. First, there is an emerging focus on career and college readiness as part of the Reauthorization of the Elementary and Secondary Education Act. The reauthorization act has placed emphases on targeting supports for teachers and schools; fostering innovation, enhancing partnerships, and improving assessments; and strengthening teacher preparation programs so that prospective teachers, including STEM teachers, have access to high-quality preparation programs.[3] Second, attention is being given to redesigning high schools in the United States. As part of this effort, focus is placed on optimizing the pace of learning for high school students, organizing internships or mentorship, involving students in project or problem-based learning, having students focus on real-world challenges, and engaging students with effective application of technology.[4] Third, there is growing momentum to build U.S. skills through community colleges. As part of President's Obama initiative, community colleges are being called upon to work with businesses, create educational partnerships, teach basic skills, meet students' needs, and develop online courses.

Each of the proposed pathways is promising, but there are critical omissions that require deeper analysis. While school-based solutions are being advanced, few, if any, community-based solutions are being offered or conceptualized. For example, solutions are not being sought to use technology to advance the literacy of youths and adults who are detached from schools and have little opportunity to take advantage of community college offerings. Additionally, ex-offenders who reenter society with insufficient literacy skills have very limited pathways to become part of the workplace because of its technology demands. Addressing these pressing issues could potentially contribute to revitalization of many urban communities. Limited transportation or fewer resources may adversely impact growth in rural communities. Neglecting large segments of urban and rural communities will have intergenerational reverberations as communities suffer from greater destabilization. This could essentially mean the end of work for segments of the population that solely rely on underground economies for their survival at the same time demand is growing for skilled workers.

There is a need to find the intersection between expedient and creative solutions to simultaneously address the needs of the U.S. economy and communities functioning at the margins. As a nation, we are challenged to use technology to grant workers employment requiring advanced technology skills. For example, there is a need to resolve how to use online mechanisms to promote literacy to those who are marginally literate, while coupling this effort to meet the needs of employers as part of an overall community development strategy. Or, appropriate conceptualizations or strategies could be framed or concretized to fund engagement project initiatives of significance in response to health-related issues in communities that mentor youths to consider science as career pathways by give them affordances to experience the impact of their efforts. These are win-win approaches that can yield significant dividends overtime that will complement some of the immediate solutions offered in West's presentation. In short, it will be wise to bring greater interdisciplinary depth to the conversation focusing on technology and workforce development, particularly those conversations focused on STEM. Literacy development has to be at the center of the conversation if the goal is to include more Americans who would be otherwise excluded because of their inability to read and write at advanced levels.

Notes

1. National Center on Education and the Economy, *Tough Choices or Tough Times: The Report of the New Commission on the Skills of the American Workforce* (San Francisco: John Wiley, 2007).

2. Darrell M. West, "Workforce Development and Technology," paper presented at the UIC Urban Forum, Chicago, Illinois, December 5, 2013. See also West's chapter of the same title in this book.

3. U.S. Department of Education, Office of Planning, Evaluation and Policy Development, *ESEA Blueprint for Reform*, Washington, D.C., 2010.

4. Nancy Hoffman, *Schooling in the Workplace: How the World's Best Vocational Education Programs Prepare Young People for Jobs and Life* (Cambridge, Mass.: Harvard Education Publishing Group, 2011).

Health Care Super Utilizers

Improving Community Care through Health Information Technologies and Data Analytics

BÉNÉDICTE CALLAN

ARIZONA STATE UNIVERSITY

INTRODUCTION

Around the United States, a small number of community health programs have exploited electronic health records (EHRs) and other health information technologies in a quest to better manage the health care of poor, uninsured, or underinsured patients who are super utilizers of health care services. These programs are heeding the call to develop new models of care that keep patients healthier and out of high-cost health environments, such as hospitals.[1] Many community initiatives seek to better integrate community and social services with medical case management. What is novel, however, is the subset of these integrated care initiatives that have succeeded in using EHRs and other electronic health information to coordinate and improve care.

In this chapter we explore which technologies and organizational structures are used by these novel health care initiatives to identify, monitor, and provide better care for health care super utilizers. What sources of information did they access? What institutions were involved or created? What policies directly or indirectly incentivized the use of novel technologies and organizational structures? What can local governments do to accelerate such information technology use for coordinated community care? The chapter is based on a literature review of the few flagship health care delivery models that use information technologies to better combine medical and social services.

New approaches to health care delivery for super utilizers are of course part of much broader changes in the social, economic, and political landscape of health care. All health care providers, serving varied populations across the country, are being challenged to find models of health care delivery that yield higher-quality care for lesser cost to the whole population, which is frequently referred to as the triple aim.[2] How to transition the U.S. health care system, or even single organizations therein, to deliver higher return on investments has been an intense policy debate in the United States for decades.[3] Proposed solutions to our health care crisis span a gamut of policy tools, including changing financial incentives for health care providers and individuals, more transparency about health care costs and health outcomes at different institutions, creating new organizational structures that facilitate communication between health care providers and create a more seamless health care experience for patients, changing the makeup of the health care workforce, promoting individual patient responsibility and behavioral changes related to nutrition and activity levels, and even urban planning. Needless to say, health experiments in health reform in the United States take myriad forms.

This chapter, however, looks specifically at the technological and organizational innovations being adopted by a still-small number of community or safety net health care providers to take advantage of various sources of patient data to improve care. For many care providers, data analytics are about developing quality metrics for the health care an institution provides. But data on patient care can also be used to help patients adhere to treatments and behaviors and thus reduce the use expensive hospital emergency department services.

Of these initiatives, we will not compare the effectiveness of the different models of care, or discuss their financial sustainability or scalability. The initiatives described here are simply recognized as alternatives to the standard model of care delivery, but we are not yet in a position to evaluate them. They are interesting experiments that address the needs of poor, often uninsured, patients with chronic conditions in a more continuous and coordinated manner.

WHAT IS THE PROBLEM WITH THE OVERUSE OF EMERGENCY CARE?

Vulnerable populations include people with (frequently multiple) chronic complex conditions, such as diabetes or asthma, whose conditions are poorly managed; the frail elderly; and people without health insurance who seek medical care only when their condition becomes acute. These diverse groups of people are more likely to resort to the use of emergency departments at hospitals for their medical conditions.

For over two decades, hospitals have been obligated to provide emergency care for any patient that visits the emergency department (ED), regardless of insurance coverage or ability to pay.[4] The expense of uncompensated ED care falls primarily on the receiving hospitals, although there are some offsetting federal funds from Medicare.[5] ED visits are more costly than regular physician visits and can result in the ordering of multiple tests and even hospital stays. Some of these ED visits might be averted if vulnerable populations had easier access to preventive, primary, or specialist care.[6]

Vulnerable populations tend to include a subpopulation of super utilizers, patients who are repeat users of emergency care. Sometimes repeat users return to the ED because the care is centralized and convenient (many hospitals, for example, have translation services). Other repeat users do so simply because their conditions are not controlled outside the hospital setting. They may be discharged without follow-up, access to other providers of care, or a support network to help them manage their conditions. They may get redundant testing at multiple hospitals.

We are living in a period of rising numbers of people with chronic conditions including diabetes, cardiac conditions, asthma, and cancer. About 60 percent of the adult U.S. population had at least one chronic condition in 2005. One in four adults have two or more chronic conditions. Chronic conditions and obesity, which is a risk factor for several chronic diseases, have added costs to the U.S. health care system.[7] But perhaps this change in the health status of Americans signals the need to shift from a health care system that has been designed for acute episodes of care to one that is designed to efficiently manage chronic conditions over time. As the president of the Center for Studying Health System Change notes, "We're pretty good at treating a heart attack, but not so good at preventing and managing the underlying heart disease that leads to that heart attack."[8]

How large a problem is the inappropriate use of emergency department care? One measure is the total charity and "bad debt" or uncompensated expenditures by hospitals. In 2011, according to the American Hospital Association, $41.1 billion of U.S. hospitals' total expenditures were for uncompensated care (5.9% of total expenditures).[9]

In 2010, the year the Affordable Care Act (ACA) was enacted, over 42 million Americans and 11 million illegal immigrants were without health insurance; in other words, over 15 percent of the population in the United States did not have regular access to affordable health care. In some southern and western states, over one in five people were not covered.[10] With the passage of the ACA the number of uninsured Americans should decrease. However, the ACA, by design, expands the number of Medicaid recipients, who statistically use emergency care at a much higher rate than the insured and even the uninsured.[11] So, even with expanded population insurance coverage, it is not clear that vulnerable populations will quickly migrate to non-ED care.[12]

The ACA is an important policy because it extends insurance coverage, encourages pay for performance, and incentivizes "accountable" models of organization for health care delivery. But it alone cannot guarantee that the health care system will suddenly be able to absorb care for the expanded Medicaid rolls or the remainder of the vulnerable populations with inadequately managed chronic conditions. Overreliance on emergency care is thus likely to continue if there are not also accompanying social and organizational changes that make outpatient care more affordable and accessible.

WHAT CAN BE DONE TO TRY TO REDUCE
THE USE OF EMERGENCY CARE?

There are many possible approaches to reducing the inappropriate use of EDs, including the creation of medical homes, community care centers, mobile doctors' offices, the broader use of telehealth technologies, and even organizational changes such as better hospital discharge instructions and follow-up. One novel solution has been to use data about patient visits to the ED in order to identify specific categories of people that might benefit from some form of intervention, be it case management, referral to a community care center or to a specialist, or social care follow-up.

Ideally, EHRs could be used to identify health care super utilizers and other categories of patients whose care is currently not well managed. EHRs include information about a patient's demographic data, conditions, medications, test results, and care received.[13] But using identifiable health records is complicated by privacy restrictions and the fact that EHR data, even unidentified meta-data, is not systematically shared among health care providers and hospitals. One community health care innovator found a way around these barriers.

In the early 2000s, Jeffrey Brenner, the founder of the Camden Coalition of Healthcare Providers located in the poorest city in New Jersey, used billing data from hospitals to create "hot-spot" maps identifying the health characteristics of individuals who ended up in Camden hospitals. Taking a page from police department targeting of crime hotspots, Brenner identified a number of interesting types of patients. For example, by looking at "locations where ambulances picked up patients with fall injuries" he discovered that "a single building in central Camden sent more people to the hospital with serious falls . . . than any other in the city, resulting in almost three million dollars in health-care bills."[14] Of those buildings in the city that accounted for the highest number and cost of hospital visits, one was a nursing home, another a low-income housing tower.

The citywide health database that Brenner created from the claims data of three Camden hospitals showed that "50 percent of Camden residents visited a local emergency department or hospital in a single year, twice the rate for the United States overall. The majority of the visits were for preventable conditions that are treatable by a primary care provider."[15] Most often people visited the ED for head colds, viral infections, ear infections, and sore throats. Thirteen percent of the patients accounted for 80 percent of hospital costs; 20 percent of the patients accounted for 90 percent of the costs.[16] Just 1 percent the Camden population accounted for 30 percent of its costs: out of 177,000 people who accessed care at Camden hospitals, fewer than eight hundred were "super-utilizers."[17]

What Brenner wanted to do was better understand the needs of the super utilizer patients in Camden. Because of privacy restrictions that limit the transfer of identified personal data, Brenner could not ask doctors to show him their patients' medical records. Instead, Brenner simply asked local doctors to refer their most problematic patients to him, and when those patients became his patients, he endeavored to find out why they accumulated such high medical costs. In 2007 he founded the Camden Coalition of Healthcare Providers, whose mission is to improve care by keeping vulnerable patients out of the hospital. The Camden coalition provides a team-based approach to the management of care for individual patients, including doctors, nurses, medical assistants, and social workers. They deliver a combination of personalized health care consultation and coordination, as well as help applying for government benefits, transportation, shelter, and other social services. Using this holistic, coordinated, and preventive approach to care, the Camden coalition was able to reduce hospital visits by 40 percent and hospital bills by 56 percent.[18] This reduction represents an enormous saving for hospitals when much of that care is uncompensated because the patients do not have health insurance or do not qualify for Medicaid or Medicare. The coalition demonstrates that it is possible to transition super utilizers into an environment where most of their care is provided by the primary-care system and a more robust social network, thus lowering the overall cost of their health care.

The Camden Coalition of Healthcare Providers was a pioneer organization using data analytics to identify which individuals were the highest consumers of health care and to create a new model of community care that combined health and social supports. Jeffrey Brenner received a MacArthur Foundation genius grant in 2013 for his innovative approach to health care. The coalition is far from alone in its objective of lowering patient care costs and providing more integrated care. Nor is it the only group interested in using data analytics. The field of health information technology is rapidly growing, making an impact in both for-profit and not-for-profit health care sectors.

Since 2010, the Office of the National Coordinator for Health Information Technology at the Department for Health and Human Services has awarded $250 million to seventeen communities across the United States that are using and exchanging claims data, clinical data, and EHRs to improve population health and measure health care quality. One recipient is the Crescent City Beacon Community in greater New Orleans, which has a chronic care management project that uses population-based registries and EHRs to risk stratify individuals and to develop care management standards and protocols that can be accessed by all participating hospitals and organizations. Another recipient is the Western New York Beacon Community, which piloted a telemonitoring project that gave diabetes patients mobile devices that regularly and electronically report vital signs to their health care providers, which makes possible early identification and intervention if a patient's diabetes is not being adequately managed. The project found that having patients monitor their own vitals improved their own ability to understand and manage their diabetes and it kept them from visiting the emergency department. Similarly, in Rochester, the Southeast Minnesota Beacon Community has two projects on childhood asthma and adult type 2 diabetes. This project is creating platforms to connect school nurses and local clinics and hospitals to share data in order to identify the local patient population and who within that population might not be receiving adequate care. In addition to data sharing, the community also created a communications system for coordinating and improving care across all care settings.[19]

HOW DO YOU GET DATA-DRIVEN
COMMUNITY CARE SOLUTIONS?

The interventions by the Camden coalition and increasingly by other community care programs are driven by a better understanding of who is the vulnerable patient population. That understanding could ultimately be derived from EHRs, but at the moment still has to be gleaned from claims data, care providers themselves, and other community partners. Those data have to be collected, collated into databases, analyzed, and shared. Obviously, the technological infrastructure that these community-based care organizations are building and using does not in itself guarantee better health care outcomes. The models of care provision matter enormously.

But setting aside the issue of how care is best delivered, how do we even build these basic information infrastructures? Surprisingly, the EHRs, databases, and information exchanges among hospital and providers are either still very new or in many instances do not yet exist. Moreover, there are several impediments to their use, some of which local organizations and governments might be able to help surmount.

What information and technologies do the Camden coalition and other community groups need to identify high-use, vulnerable patients?

First, health data for all relevant patients must be digitized so that data can be analyzed and individuals with complicated medical and social needs identified. The reality is that while EHRs have existed in some (usually partial or fragmented) form for over thirty years, it was not until the last few years that their use permeated the large majority of hospitals. Adoption of EHRs accelerated in 2009 with the passage of the federal Health Information Technology for Economic and Clinical Health (HITECH) Act, which, for all intents and purposes, mandated the use of EHRs for any provider that services the Medicare and Medicaid populations.[20] Identifying super-utilizer patients across a city or region would be much simpler if each health care provider were using EHRs.

But if a patient uses multiple health care providers, or goes to multiple hospitals, each of those institutions will have their own, separate EHRs for that single individual. So a second requirement is that the data must be sharable across providers. The HITECH Act also mandates basic data exchange. Everyone agrees that it would be beneficial if health care providers were able to see the clinically relevant clinical information about their patient. A comprehensive view of patient information helps to avoid the unnecessary duplication of tests, to improve diagnostic and prescription accuracy, and to facilitate care coordination. But the reality is that in most communities, there is no infrastructure for rapid data exchange. Much data is still exchanged via fax or paper copies, rather than digitally.

There is also a distinction to be made between the ability to transmit data across organizations and the ability to seamlessly incorporate data from different sources into EHRs. The United States and other nations have standards for diagnostic and procedural codes, laboratory tests, and prescription medications that facilitate the ability to understand the content of different EHRs. Unfortunately, the interoperability standards for merging EHR content are not yet agreed or widely used commercially. In other words, it is currently unlikely that hospitals have the capacity to automatically incorporate data generated by another EHR system. If all of a patient's care is within a single health care system, the data within that EHR are easily be kept up-to-date. But across health care systems, there are over a thousand different EHR products in use, which makes the merging of data difficult and thus care coordination and management is more complicated.[21]

Third, organizations need consent or permission to transmit and use personally identifiable health data. Health information exchanges (HIEs) must be set up across the local health care providers to facilitate the flow of data between them. HIEs are the institutional context that make it possible to share data about what patients they have (i.e., a master patient index) and what sort of data they hold (i.e., a document locator/registry). HIEs establish the rules of exchange among health data holders about their patients. Barring an HIE, data will remain siloed in separate health care provider organizations for both privacy and commercial reasons.

Depending on the state, patients will either need to consent to participate in an HIE or they might be assumed to consent unless the patient actively opts out of data sharing. A few HIEs have the capacity to let patients decide what categories of health information they are willing to share within the HIE, although most patients tend to have an all-or-none approach to data exchange. There are several different models of HIEs and much experimentation as they are still being developed (in part to meet the data exchange requirements of the HITECH Act). Broadly speaking, one can identify three models:

1. Centralized HIEs use a single clinical data repository (CDR) that is maintained by an HIE authority. HIE members (e.g., hospitals) electronically transmit agreed-upon patient health information to the CDR, where it is securely stored and continually updated.[22]
2. Federated HIEs do not have a central data repository and do not normalize or standardize the data that are remotely stored in each separate organization's EHR. The internet is used as the vehicle for moving data. To retrieve patient data, a query is sent to the HIE's patient registry, which then provides a "virtual roadmap" of where patient health records are located at different health care institutions.
3. Private HIEs can be created by a hospital system. Essentially a centralized model, it includes internal databases and referring physicians. Many accountable care organization structures are supported with private HIEs.[23]

According to the Camden Coalition of Healthcare Providers, its program uses data from the Camden Health Information Exchange, which was created in 2010 (at the instigation of the Camden coalition itself) to collaboratively share data among health care providers in the city. Three main hospitals in Camden founded the local HIE, but now over a hundred health care providers use the Camden HIE. It is a web-based system that provides real-time access to important (but limited) medical information about Camden patients (including hospital data on admissions, discharges, transfers, lab results, radiology results, medications, discharge summaries).[24] The Camden HIE also makes it possible to share more detailed clinical data among health care providers and institutions. When a specific health care record needs to be shared, that data can be securely transmitted electronically from one provider to another. The Camden HIE also includes an embedded EHR, which allows health care providers to record care management notes that can be seen by multiple health care providers in the coalition. "With patient consent, healthcare providers and social workers across the city have access to these notes and can send encrypted messages for care coordination purposes."[25]

One of the oldest HIEs is the Indiana HIE. It is a centralized HIE with a warehouse of information on over 10 million patients. IHIE connects over ninety hospitals, long-term-care facilities, rehabilitation centers, and community health clinics. It's a private entity supported by a foundation. Over twenty thousand doctors subscribe to its services (either Docs4Docs or the Indiana Network for Patient Care) allowing them to look at medical records supplied by multiple care givers. But because these sort of information exchanges require cooperation among multiple hospitals and practices, and the creation of new organizations, their financial viability is in many cases a challenge to their very creation.

Finally, someone—a community health organization, a regional provider coalition, or a private vendor—needs to analyze the aggregated health information in order to identify super utilizers and other categories of patients that might be targeted for an intervention. Data from separate health care organizations have to be accurately collated into a database, validated, and regularly updated.[26] In Camden, this aggregation is done within the HIE and can be exported "to identify additional care coordination opportunities."[27] The possibility of improving community care is inherent in these new health data collections, but the organizations and capabilities needed to do so are still immature.

POLICY CONSIDERATIONS

While it might seem obvious that hospitals and health care payers would see benefit in identifying ED super utilizers and finding more efficient care solutions to reduce their often inappropriate and costly hospital visits, the ability to use data to target patients for such interventions is in fact a fairly recent innovation.

As noted above, the use of EHRs have only become widespread since 2010, when the HITECH Act mandated their use by all providers of either Medicare or Medicaid. So, until very recently, hospitals and insurance companies primarily used their own patient data and broader medical claims data for their own analyses. Much of the data was (and still is) considered private, proprietary, and commercially sensitive. There was little appetite for sharing health information among competitive hospitals in a region. Health data were thus either owned by companies, or when shared the data was de-identified and not specific to a region.

In fact, setting up the arrangement to share health data across different providers in a region continues to be a challenge for legal, financial, and technical reasons. Legally, data transmission in HIEs must be both secure and private. Health care providers can be fined for security breaches. The Health Information Privacy and Portability Act of 1996 mandates penalties, including possible prison time for the disclosure to unauthorized parties of identified health information. The sharing of personal health information thus requires special safeguards to assure that only authorized providers and business associates have access.

In addition, it is as yet unclear whether there are strong enough incentives for groups to set up the health information exchanges that are necessary for intensive information sharing and whether they will be sustainable. There are not many centralized HIEs that have succeeded in bringing together different health care systems in a single network. The Camden Coalition of Healthcare Providers is an interesting example of federated HIEs that, by serving the vulnerable in a region, has succeeded in bringing together different hospitals willing to share limited types of data in order to reduce their often-uncompensated expenses.

There are both federal and local incentives to create HIEs and to use the shared data to improve health care outcomes for the population. What remains unclear is whether these political carrots are sufficient to incentivize the development of information exchanges regionally or nationally. While the federal government has developed Direct, its own, open-source federated model for information exchange among providers, the system will not be useful for data analytics. Created in 2010, Direct is low cost and fairly simple for the secure sharing of documents. It is essentially a secure, internet-based alternative to the fax machine for the sharing of lab results or referrals. Direct does not create a database that can be queried or used for data analytics about patients, their needs, and the quality of care they receive.

For the health information technology reasons noted above, the approach to care pioneered by the Camden Coalition of Healthcare Providers is not easy to replicate. In addition, to problems with data collection, sharing, and analysis, there are also difficulties around the health care provision model. For the Camden group, some of the coordinated care is delivered outside traditional health care provider institutions, making reimbursement problematic. However, with the creation of Medicare accountable care organizations, under the 2011 Accountable Care Act, it is hoped that some alternative models of care will be cost-effective alternatives to the current pay-for-performance care. Medical institutions that register as ACOs are eligible for an extra monthly payment to finance the coordination of care for their most chronically expensive beneficiaries. "If total costs fall more than five per cent compared with those of a matched set of control patients, the program allows institutions to keep part of the savings. If costs fail to decline, the institutions have to return the monthly payments."[28] New payment models may thus both increase incentives for shared health data use and increase the willingness to use nontraditional caregivers.

Cities and regions might be able accelerate the transition to the next generation of health care by having dialogues with their local health care providers about how to help create HIEs that serve the needs of the broader population. To better manage super utilizers, hospitals and health care providers need to be willing to share data about patients in order to identify who are the high-cost repeat users and to target interventions. There also might need to cooperate with other community groups as to what sort of analysis would be useful given the community's makeup and needs, especially in cases where care will involve a broader range of social services, such as: health coaches or social workers who visit high-cost patients at home; the establishment of dedicated primary-health care clinics in the neighborhoods with a high number of super utilizers; or networks of coordinated care givers that manage care over time.

Going forward, cities and regions might consider bringing health care providers and community groups together to discuss whether and how to build health information exchanges in their region. The participants in these exchanges will depend on the makeup of the care providers in different regions. The Department of Health and Human Services provided start-up funding for states through the State HIE Cooperative Agreement Program and to a small number of individual HIEs through the HIE Challenge Program. Nevertheless, eventually HIEs will need to be self-funded so financial considerations will be paramount, including the question of whether HIEs can help reduce health care costs or facilitate the development of new care models.

The transition to the next-generation health data exchange is already happening. Chicago announced the launch one of the largest HIEs in the United States in late 2013. The MetroChicago HIE will link eighty-nine hospitals and thousands of physicians. It will ensure comprehensive real-time data about patients and reduce test and procedure duplication. At last count, there were already close to 280 HIEs in the United States.[29] The question that remains is whether these HIEs will be closed systems, accessible only by established providers in a region, or whether they will in some ways be opened, as happened in Camden, New Jersey, so as to provide information for broader community care needs.

Notes

1. For example, see IHI Triple Aim Initiative, Institute for Healthcare Improvement, accessed February 17, 2014, www.ihi.org/.

2. Donald M. Berwick, Thomas W. Nolan, and John Whittington, "The Triple Aim: Care, Health, and Cost," *Health Affairs* 27(May 2008): 759–69, doi:10.1377/hlthaff.27.3.759.

3. The Clinton administration's failed efforts at health care reform took place in the 1990s, as did the national experiment with managed-care organizations.

4. Enacted in 1986, the Emergency Medical Treatment and Labor Act (EMTALA) requires hospitals to perform a clinical examination and to stabilize a patient if he or she presents with an emergency condition, or to arrange a transfer for that person to another facility, regardless of ability to pay.

5. The federal government provides some offsets for hospitals serving a disproportionate number of poor patients through the Medicare DSH (disproportionate-share hospital) payment adjustments, which disburses about $11 billion per year to "safety net" hospitals.

6. According to P. J. Cunningham, "About one-third of ED visits are classified as nonurgent or semi-urgent, which suggests that the care sought during many of these visits could be provided in other settings." See Peter J. Cunningham, "Medicaid/SCHIP Cuts and Hospital Emergency Department Use," *Health Affairs* 25, no. 1 (January 2008): 237–47.

7. Alwyn Cassil, "Rising Rates of Chronic Health Conditions: What Can Be Done?," Center for Studying Health System Change, Issue Brief No. 125 (November 2003), accessed February 17, 2014, www.hschange.org/.

8. Ibid.

9. American Hospital Association, *AHA Uncompensated Hospital Care Cost Fact Sheet*, 2013, accessed February 17, 2014, www.aha.org/.

10. According to the Kaiser Family Foundation, this statistic was true for Texas, Florida, Nevada, New Mexico, and Georgia. See Kaiser Family Foundation, *The Uninsured, A Primer: Key Facts about Americans Without Health Insurance*, Report No. 74561-06 (Menlo Park, Calif.: Kaiser Family Foundation, 2010).

11. Cunningham, "Medicaid/SCHIP Cuts and Hospital Emergency Department Use." "More than one-third of Medicaid/SCHIP adult enrollees had an ED visit in the previous year, compared with about 20 percent of both uninsured and privately insured adults. Overall, ED visits per adult Medicaid/SCHIP enrollee are 2.5–3 times those of privately insured and uninsured adults."

12. Rachel Zimmerman, "With Health Reform, an Increased Demand for Safety-Net Hospitals, Study Finds," August 8, 2011, http://commonhealth.wbur.org.

13. The broad adoption of EHRs holds out many promises for better health care management, but the realization of those promises is uncertain.

14. Atul Gawande, "The Hotspotters: Can We Lower Medical Costs by Giving the Neediest Patients Better Care?," *New Yorker*, January 24, 2011, accessed February 17, 2014, www.newyorker.com.

15. Robert Wood Johnson Foundation, "A Coalition Creates a Citywide Care Management System: Increasing and Improving Access to Primary and Specialty Care for Camden's Most Vulnerable Residents," January 13, 2011, accessed February 17, 2014, www.rwjf.org/en/.

16. Robert Wood Johnson Foundation, "Better Care for Super-Utilizers: A Profile of Jeffrey Brenner, MD," October 31, 2012, accessed February 17, 2014, www.rwjf.org/en/.

17. Gawande, "Hotspotters."

18. Robert Wood Johnson Foundation, "Better Care for Super-Utilizers."

19. Southeast Minnesota Beacon Program, accessed October 20, 2014, www.semnbeacon.wordpress.com.

20. Health Information Technology for Economic and Clinical Health included funding from the 2009 American Recovery and Reinvestment Act (ARRA) and provided close to $20 billion incentive payments for hospitals and physicians to use "certified" electronic health records and demonstrate their "meaningful use."

21. Mark Braunstein, *Health Informatics in the Cloud* (New York: Springer, 2013), 43.

22. Chad Johnson, Health Information Exchange: Architecture Types, Corepoint Health, February 16, 2012, accessed February 17, 2014, www.corepointhealth.com/.

23. Ibid.

24. Camden Health Information Exchange, Camden Coalition of Healthcare Providers, accessed February 17, 2014, www.camdenhealth.org.

25. "An Initiative to Reduce Unnecessary Hospital Utilization in Camden," Camden Coalition for Health Partnership, accessed February 17, 2014, www.camdenhealth.org.

26. Alternatively, it is possible to create systems that query separate EHRs for data rather than centrally collect it. This is the model for the FDA's Sentinel system of adverse drug reactions.

27. "Initiative to Reduce Unnecessary Hospital Utilization in Camden."

28. Gawande, "Hotspotters."

29. "71% of U.S. Hospitals Plan to Purchase New Health Information Exchange (HIE) Technology Solutions: 2012 CapSite U.S. Health Information Exchange (HIE) Study," September 14, 2012, PRWeb, www.prweb.com.

The Potential Global Impact of Smart Technology on Health Services

DISCUSSANT: MICHELLE STOHLMEYER RUSSELL

Technology in health care is such a vast topic that our esteemed panel spent dinner the evening before the forum trying to define which portions we wanted to discuss. We agreed that we should focus on the opportunity of technology to improve the quality of care. We agreed that we should focus on the challenges, but highlight how the evolving landscape is lessening some of those issues. We agreed that we should end the panel discussion with our perspectives on how policy can help accelerate the transformation of health care and ease its implementation.

The panel consisted of individuals with a complement of backgrounds: Don Bisbee, senior vice president from Cerner Corporation, brought the perspective of technology and devices. Bénédicte Callan, a professor at Arizona State University, had an insightful view of the social and political implications. Dr. Jerry Krishnan from the University of Illinois highlighted the potential of technology to improve outcomes. Dr. Julio Silva from Rush University Medical Center brought the perspective of applying technology in the emergency room, but also shared his view on the medical Direct program of the MetroChicago Information Exchange.

The group discussed a number of the challenges that create barriers to more effective use of technology, including

- fragmented data,
- concerns about patient privacy, and
- challenges with patient education.

FRAGMENTED DATA

Clearly one significant challenge is the vast number and sources of patient data. Focusing on hospitals also, vast amounts of data are generated annually across 35 million hospital discharges, 100 million outpatient department visits, and 130 million emergency department visits. This expands exponentially with expansion from the hospital into physician offices and clinics. This explosion of health-related data occurs in the home and even on the go—whether it is a smart scale or a Fitbit. There is a vast array of data that could be relevant to the delivery of care, but it resides in pockets across the spectrum.

Nevertheless there are examples of progress within Chicago on interconnectivity. For example, the MetroChicago Information Exchange will be one of the nation's largest unified health information exchanges (HIEs), securely managing protected health information for patients throughout the greater Chicago area, with plans to share data across thirty-four Chicago-area hospitals with implementation starting in the first quarter of 2014.

In her white paper for the forum, Bénédicte Callan highlighted the sharing of data to manage emergency room usage within a very small population. The Camden Coalition of Healthcare Providers identified a set of super utilizers who were using emergency departments across this New Jersey city as a substitute for other needs. By developing a coordinated care model that incorporated personalized health care consultation and coordination, as well as support for applying for government benefits, transportation, shelter and other social services, the coalition reduced hospital visits by 40 percent and hospital bills by 56 percent.

PATIENT PRIVACY

Many questions arose during the discussion about patient privacy. One of the advantages of the Health Insurance Portability and Accountability Act (HIPAA) is that everyone agrees that a patient owns his/her data. However, the usage of such data creates challenges. There are questions with how patients access the data; the increased utilization of patient portals is one contributor to patients' access. Even if patients can access the data, is it secure?

The issues with data security are seen as manageable, with the more challenging component being human error and misconduct. Some of the largest breaches of patient data have involved stolen back-up tapes or stolen computers. Civil penalties for HIPAA violations and range from $100,000 to over $50,000 per violation. Criminal penalties can be levied against those who knowingly obtain or disclose personal health information, including significant fines ($50,000–$250,000) and imprisonment.

PATIENT EDUCATION

With the rise of technology, patients have expanding access to data but often are not equipped to fully understand it or to identify which information is relevant to their condition and which information may be untrue. A powerful use of technology is that providers can help educate their patients. Technology is also allowing connectivity across patients to enable peer-based learning and support through models like the online research network PatientsLikeMe.

A required critical enabler is health literacy: a patient's ability to understand, interpret, and use health-related information. Research has shown that lower health literacy leads to increased expenditures and poorer outcomes. The University of Illinois's efforts to develop patient videos that provide valid, scientifically based information on medications and/or patient conditions that are accessible is one example of an organization working to improve health literacy. Over time, a library of content will be created by trusted sources that can be used for ready access using mobile platforms like cell phones.

While there was acknowledgment of these challenges, the group was excited about progress across several dimensions, in particular

- increased collaboration,
- reimbursement that is tied to outcomes and more patient focused, and
- policies that reward investments in technology.

INCREASED COLLABORATION

Clearly, there is a move toward collaboration, and we see this in how agencies are funding trials. One recent example of this in the Chicago area is the PCORI (Patient-Centered Outcomes Research Institution) grant that was awarded to a collaborative effort across ten institutions. The evolution of this grant application tells the story of an evolving Chicago health community. The request for proposal was issued in spring 2013 for technology platforms that support patient-centered research. When three sites in the region indicated their interest, the Illinois Medical District Commission and Chicago

Community Trust helped bring them together to submit a single application from the Alliance of Chicago's FQHCs, a number of academic medical centers (at Loyola University, North Shore Community College, Northwestern University, Rush University, the University of Illinois, and the University of Chicago), the Veterans Affairs hospitals (Hines and Jesse Brown), and Cook County Health and Hospital Systems. In December 2013, $6.99 million was awarded to this effort, and the Chicago Area Patient Centered Clinical Outcomes Research Network (CAPriCORN) project is ongoing.

REIMBURSEMENT THAT IS OUTCOME-BASED AND MORE PATIENT-FOCUSED

There is a shift from episodic care focused at the site of care to continuous, preventive care that is focused on the patient. This shift is being reinforced by changes in payment and reimbursement that are forcing hospitals to be more attentive to what happens to patients outside of the four walls of the hospital. With the introduction of the CMS Hospital Readmission Reduction Program in 2012, the incentives are aligned to ensure that providers are actively managing care outside of the hospital to prevent readmissions. This requires interconnectivity of technology across multiple settings of care.

In addition to negative incentives from readmission penalties, there are positive incentives being driven from Managed Medicaid and Managed Medicare. Research has shown that these programs can reduce costs while increasing the quality of care. In research by the Boston Consulting Group (BCG) on alternative care models, we found that patients enrolled in Medicare Advantage (MA) plans had better outcomes than those participating in traditional fee-for-service Medicare. MA patients had lower single-year mortality rates, shorter average hospital stays, and fewer readmissions. They also received high levels of recommended preventive care and had fewer disease-specific complications. MA plans are a great example of using technology to manage care to reduce costs and improve outcomes.

POLICIES THAT REWARD INVESTMENTS IN TECHNOLOGY

One example of the use of government policy to drive behavior is the success of the Health Information Technology for Economic and Clinical Health (HITECH) Act and its impact on meaningful use of electronic health records (EHRs). The goal is to show that institutions are using EHR technology in ways that can be used to measure improvements in quality. Stage 1 certification requires the ability to capture data in a structured way and share it within an institution. Stage 2 requires data sharing across multiple settings (e.g., with another institution) and requires more patient-controlled data.

Many challenges remain, and there is opportunity for further utilization of policy to drive adoption and changes. The group discussed the need for changes in payment models and clinician incentives to educate patients. They also discussed the potential role of government in validating information. However, the challenge of defining what is clinical information was readily acknowledged. It is also critical to demonstrate sustainable improvements in outcomes with a reasonable return. One of the most significant concerns expressed about the mandates of the HITECH Act was the associated spend on health care IT, with forecasts that the spend by U.S. health care organizations will be greater than $30 billion in 2014.

We believe that the coupling of technology with continued experimentation with care delivery models and increased collaboration can help drive progress. We are excited with the progress demonstrated by entities like CAPriCORN and MetroChicago Information Exchange, and we believe the combination of connectivity and patient-centered care can drive a transformation. There will be many "growing pains" as we evolve from a system of fragmented data and disparate systems to one of interconnectivity that is patient-centered. However, we are optimistic about the future and believe that metropolitan areas will lead and benefit from this evolution.

PART THREE

SYNTHESIS AND RECOMMENDATIONS

Plugged In

Connecting Citizens in Chicago and Beyond

STEPHANIE TRUCHAN

UIC COLLEGE OF URBAN PLANNING

AND PUBLIC AFFAIRS

At the turn of the twentieth century, about 20 percent of the world's population lived in urban areas. This number has since risen to over 50 percent. According to a World Health Organization projection, approximately 70 percent of the world's population will live in cities by 2050, with the most rapid urban population growth occurring in developed countries. Population increases bring about a whole host of new issues ranging from public health, to housing, to economic development. And while there are many different ways to address these new issues, one thing most people can agree on is that technology is going to be the key to ensuring long-term success of urban centers.

In today's "plugged-in" world, the real challenge cities face is identifying who has access to technology and who does not. The ultimate goal is to make sure no citizen is left out. In order to keep up with changing times, cities must adopt the most efficient technologies and adapt to the need for continuous growth and innovation. While technology alone will not raise economic or living standards, it can provide the stability and equality that cities need in order to compete in an ever tech-reliant world.

University of Illinois at Chicago chancellor Paula Allen-Meares's welcome remarks opened the 2013 Urban Forum and set the stage for a day of conversations about how cities can best connect to their citizens and to one another.

UIC has become a major player in the conversations about the urban landscape, exemplifying the interactive role public research universities can have in advancing the quality of life in and helping bring prosperity to their cities. With a growing emphasis on education, it is important that universities, especially urban ones, continue to reach out to their communities and become active anchor institutions.

Cook County Board president and keynote speaker Toni Preckwinkle stressed how impactful technology has been to both the county and the City of Chicago. Rather than investing in updated technology, the county historically has spent money trying to keep its outdated technology running. Today, the county is taking a tech-driven approach in order to become a major player in the region and beyond. A new emphasis on open data and mobile technologies is propelling Cook County and Chicago into the twenty-first century.

CREATING INFORMED COMMUNITIES: ACCESSIBLE TECHNOLOGIES TO HELP ENHANCE THE QUALITY OF LIFE

To help better understand what cities are doing to create informed communities, WBEZ's Natalie Moore sat down with Brian Kelly, Quintiles's president of Payer and Provider Solutions; John Tolva, former chief technology officer for the City of Chicago; Susana Vasquez, executive director at Local Initiatives Support Corporation (LISC) in Chicago; and Tim Wisniewski, director of civic technology for the City of Philadelphia.

Moore began the conversation by breaking down some of the key themes from the 2013 Urban Forum's overview white paper by Karen Mossberger. In today's high-tech society, it is difficult to imagine not being connected, especially in highly urbanized areas of the country. We often associate "dead zones" with rural, sparsely populated areas of the country. But approximately 30 percent of the population in Chicago and across the country does not have broadband at home, and 15 percent of the population does not use the internet at all. This does not necessarily mean that these individuals live in "dead zones." It means that they do not have the *means* to access a reliable, wired, internet connection.

But access to information technology is not just limited to citizens. Increased technology and easier access to it has been shown to bolster economic development by increasing the quality and quantity of information shared between industries and municipalities. Readily available public health data have the potential to spark new developments in the health care field. And government transparency and citizen participation are fueled by open data and easy-to-access municipal information.

Each panelist provided insight into what his or her municipality or organization is doing to help connect citizens to technology and create a more resilient city.

WHAT IS BEING DONE IN YOUR CITY OR WITHIN YOUR ORGANIZATION TO HELP CONNECT CITIZENS TO TECHNOLOGY? As the City of Chicago's former chief technology officer, John Tolva said he is most proud of Mayor Rahm Emanuel's influence in changing the culture of decision making in the city, which is now being informed by data. This approach is being woven into how the city is addressing the issue of technology and connectivity. He noted that smartphone penetration is high in both Chicago and across the country, and while mobile technology allows individuals to connect to the internet, it is an emaciated version of access.

To combat reliance on mobile web surfing, Chicago mayor Rahm Emmanuel is working on a number of initiatives within in the city's Broadband Challenge. He is working with providers to lower the cost of access and utilizing freight lines, sewer lines, Chicago Transit Authority tunnels, and other unused capacities to build a third access option into neighborhoods.

Ultimately, technology is not about cost or access. It is about rationale and the reasoning behind using technology. To help individuals understand why they should be online, the city and other community organizations are promoting digital literacy through programs that teach citizens the importance of knowing how to find and use data.

Tolva recalled that the first thing he wanted to do when he began working as chief technology officer was to "open" the data. Opening the data involves releasing maps, geographic information system data, and statistical information about the city to the general public. This type of information can include anything from financial and budget numbers, to crime rates, to environmental statistics, to medical data and practice.

The city was far behind in this capacity, but officials did not want open data to just be about transparency. Tolva went a step further and published the vital signs of the city in an effort to increase accountability and promote data analysis and economic development. Making data available in context is entirely different from simply making data available. Chicago's efforts were centered on showing citizens where money is being spent, where crime is occurring, and where development is happening.

In Chicago and in other cities with open data, there are many citizens who have access to the data but lack the statistical background necessary to interpret it. Therefore, much of this information has only been analyzed by academics and professionals with specialized knowledge. Digital literacy programs can help ordinary citizens better understand municipal data, but until this literacy becomes widespread, the city is working to bring the data to the populace by developing more user-friendly tables, charts, and maps. These graphical interpretations of the data are easier to read than the raw data and allow comparisons, contrasts, and trends to stand out.

Tim Wisniewski joined the conversation to bring a comparative perspective of technology and connectivity from the city of Philadelphia. He said that about 41 percent of Philadelphia residents do not have wired broadband internet at home, although many citizens have access to smartphones.

Philadelphia mayor Michael Nutter has taken two steps to combat the lack of wired connectivity and reliance on mobile technology. His initial project was the Keyspot Program, which created technology-enabled community centers. These centers are essentially computer labs that provide free internet access and training to educate people on the importance of being connected and to improve their digital literacy. The city is also targeting the mobile aspect of connectivity by building mobile web apps. These cross-platform applications will function on smartphones, laptops, and tablets. Mobile technology is quickly becoming the most common way people are accessing data, so this mobile-centric strategy is being incorporated into all future app development.

Because he is the first person to hold the director of civic technology position, Wisniewski said he was able to start with a clean slate and essentially go in any direction he chose. In addition to better mobile access, the city is also working on language access, electronic signature platforms, and open-data initiatives.

As has Chicago, Philadelphia has partnered with community organizations to help promote access and digital literacy. Many of the Keyspot Program community centers are operated by nonprofit, educational, and community organizations.

Susana Vasquez next addressed the audience about the Smart Communities Program in Chicago. This program began as a recommendation from the 2007 Mayor Advisory Council under Mayor Richard M. Daley. The report contained many recommendations, among which was to create a pilot program to increase digital literacy. In addition to cost, access, and difficulty, Vasquez said that privacy concerns were another major factor in why many citizens were not getting online.

Because the Local Initiatives Support Corporation (LISC) was already well-known in many neighborhoods, the organization was central in the development of the Smart Communities Program. LISC began with the question of how technology access could help improve the quality of life for residents. To accomplish that, LISC implemented neighborhood-driven plans and had technology organizers begin creating social networks within the neighborhoods and telling residents about the new array of resources available.

LISC also helps operate technology centers for working families that focus on education and employment services. These centers have computer labs with technology trainers who assist residents in using these services. The organization has helped bring digital news to neighborhoods through community newspapers, and they have assisted private businesses in developing their digital presence. LISC relies on community residents to help spread the word about digital literacy programs by telling their neighbors what they have learned from being online and how other citizens can have the same experience.

These technology centers can be found in Woodlawn, Pilsen, Auburn-Gresham, Chatham, and Englewood—neighborhoods in which LISC already had a presence. Englewood Codes and Teamwork Englewood are using social networking to spur innovation in Englewood. Pilsen is using technology to create a new, neighborhood-centered media outlet that focuses on the positive development occurring in the community. These programs are attracting increasing numbers of residents because they provide a way for community members to utilize their talents and learn something new, all while creating a positive image of their neighborhoods.

Brian Kelly provided a private-sector view of how technology is bolstering the health care industry. The world's largest provider of biopharmaceutical development, Quintiles assists pharmaceutical companies in developing new drugs, carrying out clinical trials, and bringing new drugs to health care markets.

In the past, it was relatively simple to find drug trial participants. Pharmaceutical companies would often have upward of thirty thousand participants, and the company would know the side effects of the drug. Today, pharmaceutical companies have access to more information, including genetic markers, so they need to be more specific in their recruiting. Using technology to market drug trials gives companies the breadth they need to reach a large base of individuals from varying demographics. Additionally, better technology allows these companies to follow patients for longer periods of time, thus enabling them to monitor the long-term side effects of the drugs.

The digital component of health care has been in place since 2007 with the initial development of Mediguard. Mediguard grew out of patients' desire to enroll in a Listserv that would relay information about new drugs and changes to drug trials over time. Over time, these listservs have turned into more focused digital communities, still dedicated to providing patients with pertinent information.

WHAT ARE THE OPPORTUNITIES AND CHALLENGES FOR INDIVIDUALS WHO RELY SOLELY ON A MOBILE DEVICE FOR INTERNET ACCESS? More and more people are getting online using smartphones and other mobile devices. While this type of technology is good for on-the-go updates, it provides an emaciated version of access. Mobile devices assist individuals in accessing basic internet features, such as social media and email, but these devices are limited in their capabilities. For example, many mobile phones and personal tablets will not load flash-based websites. Individuals who rely solely on a mobile device for internet access have been shown to do less online and also have fewer technology skills. But this does not mean mobile technology does not have its merits.

Many public health issues are linked to a lack of information. Citizens cannot make informed decisions if they do not have access to public health resources. Cities are now looking at this problem and using low-technology initiatives like text messages to spread information. It is older technology that remains ubiquitous because of the widespread use of mobile phones.

To understand the opportunities and challenges of relying on mobile technology, we can look to the organization and outreach utilized by the Affordable Care Act. Administrators are using simple tools to track information about the individuals being touched by the Affordable Care Act. Most of these people prefer to be contacted via text message. Although these text messages have the ability to reach a large audience, they pose in issue in collecting the necessary data. Individuals can only send back short blurbs or one-word responses. Given the nature of these responses, only very basic data can be gleaned from them.

One major challenge with text messages and especially apps is the potential for compartmentalization, or limited access to information that may prove useful to the greater community of necessary in order to perform certain tasks. There is still a need to make people aware of applications that may prove useful to them. To fully combat compartmentalization, cities need to make sure that citizens learn how to use these applications. And in order to do that, cities need to move their touchpoints out into the environment. By decentralizing the interaction points within a city, municipal governments can establish a system that is more in tune with how citizens naturally interact.

WHAT IS BEING DONE TO BRIDGE THE GAP BETWEEN THE APPS THAT TECH GU-RUS PRODUCE AND WHAT IS ACTUALLY NEEDED IN THE AVERAGE NEIGHBOR-HOOD? Silicon Valley technology gurus are constantly releasing new apps, but they do not fully understand what cities need in order to reach citizens. In order to better meet citizens' needs, both cities and developers alike can utilize civic-user testing groups—the act of going into neighborhoods and recruiting citizens to test apps based on their needs and provide feedback.

Philadelphia is one city that is seeing a gap between what app developers are pushing and what citizens need. Developed by the city, the My Philly Rising app was not intended to solve the bigger problem, but rather to help the people and programs that are trying to solve the problem by complementing the efforts already made by app developers. The app allows content generators to publish neighborhood events and information on community resources, facilities, and services. Each neighborhood has a separate section of the app that features information unique and pertinent to that area of the city.

Chicago is working with youths and schools to bridge the technology gap, and adults are also partaking because they want to be involved in what their kids are doing. The city is realigning the school system to focus on science, technology, engineering, and math (STEM) curriculums and establishing a base level of technical fluency. As most of the white papers for this event suggest, cities and metropolitan regions drive the national economy. Since the economy is becoming dominated by STEM jobs, new employees need to have a good foundation in how technology works in order to be competitive candidates in the job market.

Mayor Rahm Emanuel assisted in establishing five high schools that are partnered with the private sector. Their curriculum offers a six-year program that allows students to obtain both a high school diploma and an associate's degree, which puts them first in line for tech jobs.

In Chicago, this approach is not just tried; it is true, especially in the case of the Smart Chicago program. This model is effective because neighbor-hoods matter in Chicago, and the city strives to make sure that broadband is on par. In this program specifically, Chicago is providing an innovative example by combining technology and community development.

WHAT INNOVATIONS HAVE YOU SEEN IN OTHER CITIES? Philadelphia created a program called Big Ideas PHL, which is trying to engage local vendors in a transparent way using modern technology as opposed to using older con-tracts. This platform is giving the city the ability to post and get responses from a variety of vendors, and it is being rolled out in other cities in the area.

Code for America, a national, municipality-driven program, provides civic commons where cities can post open-source apps that can then be adopted by other cities. The nature of the program allows innovation to flourish in a low-risk setting but also creates a competitive technology-centric civic marketplace.

WHAT DO YOU HEAR FROM PEOPLE ABOUT WHAT THEY WANT? In short, citizens want access to technology and the internet, and social media has influenced that conversation. Chicago and Cook County prefer a two-way conversation, but both the city and the county follow social media trends to see who is talking about what, and they study how to use those channels in unique ways. The City of Chicago government believes that it is up to the public to find out the best use for municipal data, and the city is serving as a platform for innovation.

Philadelphia, on the other hand, is using mediators outside the government to help bridge the gap between open data and the general public. A local investigative journalism agency, one such mediator, broke down tax data from the Philadelphia Actual Value initiative into an understandable map within hours of release of the data.

On the health care side, people want communities. When patients can be engaged in a community before even engaging in a clinical trial, they are much more receptive to new information and more likely to participate in the program.

The health care industry is spending a lot of time trying to figure out how to establish these communities. Health care professionals and consultants are working with patient advocacy groups and other stakeholders to get patients involved and committed through initiatives like the Annual Health Data Palooza. This program takes federal health care data and puts them in the public's hands. Having access to data is spurring innovators to create apps and sparking a sense of community among patients.

As much as technology has helped the health care industry, there is no substitute for feet on the ground to drive the creation of better care and lower costs. With the next wave of patients, the big question is how to drive behavioral changes. This is one issue in which technology is really having an impact.

WHAT CAN WE DO LOCALLY FOR BETTER COORDINATION AND IMPLEMENTATION? The most important thing is to acknowledge reality. There is a trend toward mobile technology, so apps and platforms need to be mobile friendly, both in the public and the private sector.

If you start with people, there is also a resource allocation question. Philanthropy is still trying to figure out its priorities, and the private sector needs nudging. As cities start funding plans and programs, it's important for them to invest in strategic neighborhood infrastructure.

Individuals and cities also need to figure out how to work together better to establish communities of trust where people are comfortable sharing their data. The public and private sectors both have to personalize their approaches, and there is room to do that only if individuals trust that they can be included in these efforts.

Ultimately, cities need to start with trust, not technology. Cities need to start with people first, and then let technology follow. By being part of the conversation at the street level, cities are confident they can help close the connectivity gap.

ADVANCED TECHNOLOGY DRIVING OUR WORKFORCE: THE GROWING EFFECT OF TECHNOLOGY ON TOMORROW'S JOBS

Data from the U.S. Bureau of Labor Statistics shows that the information industry is the nation's fastest-growing business sector, which is why adapting to the digital economy is crucial. Despite the increase in high-tech and STEM jobs, the United States lacks sufficient numbers and training of employees in these fields. As the baby boomer generation ages, the nation's workforce also faces large numbers of retirees. If younger generations do not have the knowledge and skills necessary to adapt to a shift in the economy and if positions in high-tech industries then remain unfilled, the U.S. economy could look very different in the coming decades.

WBEZ's Niala Boodhoo, along with Mark Harris, president and chief executive officer of the Illinois Science and Technology Coalition, Jeff Malehorn, president and chief executive officer of World Business Chicago, Theresa Mintle, president and chief executive officer of the Chicagoland Chamber of Commerce, and Ted Smith, chief of economic growth and innovation for the City of Louisville, sat down to sort out how we as a nation are training our future STEM employees and adapting our cities to keep up with the changing economy.

HOW IMPORTANT IS IT TO CHICAGO'S ECONOMY TO HAVE A TECH-SAVVY WORKFORCE OF HIGH-TECH COMPANIES BASED HERE? According to both Jeff Malehorn and Ted Smith, it is essential to have high-tech jobs and a tech-savvy workforce—doing without either is just not an option. Technology is the future for every business, and it is absolutely Chicago's future, too. It is important that this trickles down into neighborhoods and small businesses throughout the country.

Today's economy is knowledge based. High-wage, high-value jobs are where forward-thinking cities need to be focusing. If Chicago and other major cities are not able to move the workforce, essentially the working backbone of the country, into the future, these cities will be trading with an entirely different—and infinitely less valuable—set of knowledge-backed currency.

In Chicago, for example, World Business Chicago is helping the city and region to rally around moving the state's economic engine in the right direction. The goal is to ensure that Chicago continues to be a great global business city, and officials are working through strategies with various organization and business partners to help make that happen.

HOW HAS TRAINING A TECH-SAVVY WORKFORCE WORKED IN LOUISVILLE? According to Ted Smith, Louisville has a much smaller economic market than Chicago. Industries define the community. Louisville recognizes that GE, Ford, UPS, and other big businesses have shaped the way the business environment in the city works, and the city understands the need to work with the assets it has. There is a major focus on being a good partner to the future of those industries.

The conversation in Louisville has also turned to colocation startups. These types of businesses are so important because companies are hungry for that entrepreneurial maker-doer person. To harness the power of the entrepreneurial community, Louisville took the model of STEM jobs and developed Code Louisville, an open-community initiative that asks coders and hackers to be mentors. This type of community engagement promotes digital literacy and awareness and promote STEM fields.

MANUFACTURERS EMPHASIZE THEIR NEED FOR WORKERS WHO CAN PERFORM ADVANCED MANUFACTURING. HOW DO WE BRIDGE THE GAP BETWEEN THE NEEDS OF ADVANCED MANUFACTURING AND HAVING A WORKFORCE TRAINED IN THE FIELD? Illinois Innovation Partners is just one of a number of organizations trying to bridge the gap. Computer occupations make up the biggest STEM segment occupations in Chicago, and in order to fill those positions, schools need to graduate more students with STEM degrees. Demand for these jobs is expected to rise by 60 percent, and about 93 percent of these jobs will require an advanced education. It's important to note that not all of these jobs will require an advanced *degree*—some may simply require advanced credentials that can be obtained without a traditional four-year college degree.

The City of Chicago has been a partner to redesign how the City Colleges of Chicago system works. The community colleges have been redesigned to focus on a skills area, but this shift was not just a matter of designating which campus will focus on what skill. Administrators went directly to employers and asked about the skills gap, and these employers designed the curriculum at specific campuses so that students who graduate are fully qualified for a certain job.

The community college system is helping to bring higher education to the table, too. Students from the community colleges can go on to four-year colleges in the city to earn higher degrees. This system has turned around the way the City of Chicago trains people for jobs.

Universities also are reinventing themselves as economic engines for the state. States need to utilize these tools and unlock their potential. Entrepreneurship has historically been confined to the business school. We are now seeing place-based centers that have innovation nodes across the campus, and these innovation centers carry that mindset across disciplines. The goal is not to have everyone be an entrepreneur, but to bring innovation to all sectors and all levels.

HOW SIMILAR IS THE DIGITAL MANUFACTURING INITIATIVE TO THE INNOVATION NODES? Large corporations and small startups are coming together. Startups need functional guidance and operating systems to become large companies, and large companies need entrepreneurship to keep going. In twenty years, about 40 percent of Fortune 500 companies will no longer exist. To stay relevant and reduce the risk of failure, large companies need to think outside their walls about how they innovate. They need to collaborate with these smaller startups and form partnerships around these nodes of innovation. There has been a decline in corporate research and development nationally, but Illinois companies still show more than $16 billion R&D funds. The state is making an effort to put even more money into research and development.

HOW DO R&D AND INNOVATIVE COLLABORATION WORK FOR SMALL AND ME-DIUM-SIZED BUSINESS? Small and medium-sized businesses support a large portion of the economy's job creation. Every day, business owners ask local chambers of commerce for help to connect with people who are successful in their business endeavors.

Chambers of commerce can bring larger partners together with small businesses to give confidential and preliminary information on all kinds of important tools, such as cloud computing and open data. Exchanging ideas can help large and small businesses alike to think outside the box and to learn to utilize new strategies for everything from marketing to product development.

Chicago specifically has opened data for people to access and use, and this has proven useful to small and midsized businesses. The city also has put time and energy into working with partners to make access to Wi-Fi more readily available and less expensive. The State of Illinois is currently developing a state-level plan for economic development. There is a lot of talk about education, but it is important to remember that sometimes businesses need a nudge, as well.

WHAT CAN WE DO TO HELP EVERY STUDENT IN CHICAGO ACHIEVE A COLLEGE DEGREE? In order to get everyone through college, communities need to help girls and minorities into the sciences. This interest needs to be an extended pathway that starts in elementary schools.

One way to spark this interest is to look at the set of jobs that young people can do. Having young people earn money is a first step toward forming future entrepreneurs. It is also important to look at a broad range of investments, such as summer programs and examples of schools that focus on advanced manufacturing.

Chicago's goal in restructuring the school system was to interest both males and females in science and to graduate a higher percentage of students. There is also a push to create more experiential learning experiences in high schools.

Chicago schools have a mentor-matching engine. This engine is a virtual platform that allows students at the hub to post questions and the mentors on the other end to respond. By supplementing classroom education in this way, students can see a career progression for themselves that they may not have previously thought of.

WHAT RESPONSIBILITY DOES THE BUSINESS COMMUNITY HAVE TO ADVOCATE FOR THIS CHANGE? Most businesses think they have a huge responsibility to get involved. We are learning how the habits of the past several years affect the way people approach work. The current generation skipped the whole childhood work experience, but people are beginning to tweak the way they are raising their kids to help them be more skill-savvy and learn those skills early in life.

There is an expectation in Chicago that CEOs need to become involved and to invest in community and economic development through the lens of innovation. The business community is aware of the future being tied to technology, and they are investing in that. There is collaboration going on at every level to make sure we are focused on moving in the right direction.

A remark from Jeff Malehorn perfectly sums up the morning's discussions. He believes that sharing practices is key. Cities need to come together to lift up the country and drive economic growth. It is not just about corporate success; it is all about businesses. It is about a partnership between civic and academic institutions and business communities, and this is something that is possible in all cities.

What's Next?

The white paper authors, panel discussants, and moderators identified, analyzed, and debated the issues surrounding digital literacy and digital citizenship. While these issues cannot be solved in one afternoon, the UIC Urban Forum participants set forth a broad range of potential policy suggestions for the integration of technology and citizenship.

AS JANE FOUNTAIN PHRASES IT, "ATTEND TO THE DIGITAL DIVIDE."

- Install inclusive technology solutions that can be accessed by individuals of all races and income levels.
- Look at connectivity at the neighborhood level and directly address the needs of citizens.
- Educate citizens on the importance and value of digital literacy, and show them how being tech-savvy can enhance their lives.
- Open the data and provide citizens with the skills and resources they need in order to accurately interpret and successfully use it.
- With regard to government, emphasize the importance of using data to inform policy decisions.

BRIDGE THE GAP BETWEEN ADVANCED MANUFACTURING AND THE SPECIALIZED KNOWLEDGE IT TAKES TO WORK IN THESE JOBS.

- Stress the importance of acquiring the necessary skills—this does not have to mean also acquiring a traditional college degree.
- Improve science, technology, engineering, and mathematics (STEM)

curriculums in elementary, middle, and high schools to provide students with the basic skills they need to succeed in an advanced-level STEM education program.

- Attract more women and minorities to the STEM fields by creating a pathway from elementary schools.
- Change STEM to STEAM (science, technology, engineering, arts, and mathematics) and focus on a range of literacies instead of only the technical ones.
- Encourage the sharing of resources and knowledge by bringing large corporations and small start-ups together.

ADDRESS THE MYRIAD ISSUES SURROUNDING THE HEALTH CARE FIELD AND PATIENT DATA.

- Bring citizens' groups and health care providers together to determine whether and how to build health information exchanges in communities.
- Promote health care literacy and invest in programs and opportunities that will enhance a patient's ability to understand and apply health data.
- Build digital communities where patients can access data relating to specific conditions and interact with other patients in similar situations.
- Encourage continued collaboration between agencies when funding health care trials with an emphasis on sharing technology and data.
- Address the issue of patient privacy by allowing patients to access their health data through patient technology portals.

Contributors

RANDY BLANKENHORN is executive director of CMAP, the Chicago Metropolitan Agency for Planning (www.cmap.illinois.gov). Under his leadership, CMAP developed and is now guiding the implementation of GO TO 2040, metropolitan Chicago's first comprehensive regional plan in more than a century. Blankenhorn and CMAP staff work closely with seven counties, 284 municipalities, and scores of stakeholder groups to implement the plan's strategies for aligning public policies and investments. Prior to joining CMAP in 2006, Blankenhorn was bureau chief of urban program planning for the Illinois Department of Transportation, coordinating activities of the fourteen metropolitan planning organizations across Illinois.

BÉNÉDICTE CALLAN is a clinical professor in the College of Health Solutions at Arizona State University. She is interested in the social and political implications of new health technologies. She was the Sid Richardson Fellow and Lecturer at the LBJ School of Public Affairs at the University of Texas, Austin, from 2009 to 2011. For twelve years Callan was an official at the Organization of Economic Cooperation and Development in Paris, France. Callan received her PhD from the University of California–Berkeley in political science and her bachelor's degree from Yale University in biology and East Asian studies.

JANE E. FOUNTAIN is a professor of political science and public policy as well as the director of the National Center for Digital Government at the University of Massachusetts Amherst. She is a leading researcher and a frequent keynote speaker on technology and government globally. Her latest work focuses on technology and cross-agency collaboration. Fountain is a past chair of the World Economic Forum Global Agenda Council on the Future of Government and has been a council member since its inception. She is an elected fellow of the National Academy of Public Administration and an appointed member of the Commonwealth of Massachusetts Governor's Council on Innovation.

CHEN-YU KAO is a PhD student in the School of Public Affairs at Arizona State University. Her research interests include organizational theory, organizational pathology, government-citizen relations, citizen participation, deliberative policy making, as well as the opportunities and challenges that information technology brings to the above areas. More specifically, her current studies explore how citizen participation affects administrative and policy decision making. She also explores how different aspects of organizational theory, through public or nonprofit organizations, could facilitate or inhibit meaningful citizen participation.

SANDEE KASTRUL is the president and cofounder of i.c.stars, an organization that provides inner-city youth with training in technology, leadership, and business skills. Working in education for more than two decades, Kastrul's career highlights include implementing a professional development program with the Harold Washington College Career Center, designing a comprehensive science and civics interactive program for Jobs for Youth, developing diversity trainings and curriculum strategies for the Illinois Resource Center and the Merrillville School Corporation, as well as creating artist-in-residency programs for several performing-arts organizations in Chicago.

KAREN MOSSBERGER is professor and director of the School of Public Affairs at Arizona State University. Her research interests include urban policy, digital inequality, e-government, and broadband. Recent books include *Digital Cities: The Internet and the Geography of Opportunity* (Oxford University Press 2012, with C. Tolbert and W. Franko), and the *Oxford Handbook of Urban Politics* (2012, with S. Clarke and P. John). Mossberger is evaluating the Smart Communities Program, a digital inclusion initiative in five Chicago neighborhoods, with support from the John D. and Catherine T. MacArthur Foundation. Current work on a broadband data repository and conference is funded by the National Science Foundation.

DANIEL X. O'NEIL is the executive director of the Smart Chicago Collaborative, a civic organization devoted to making lives better in Chicago through technology. Smart Chicago was founded by the City of Chicago, the John D. and Catherine T. MacArthur Foundation, and the Chicago Community Trust. Prior to his work at Smart Chicago, O'Neil cofounded EveryBlock, where he was responsible for uncovering new data sets through online research and working with local governments. He has worked in the open-government and open-data movement since 2004, creating technology, advocating for and writing policy, and working to improve how communities use data to make decisions and improve conditions.

MICHELLE STOHLMEYER RUSSELL is a partner and managing director at the Boston Consulting Group (BCG), leading the Healthcare Practice for the Great Lakes & Canada System. She is also a member of the People and Organization Practice. Russell focuses much of her work on academic medical centers, hospital systems, and payers. She has previous experience in the areas of strategy, mergers and acquisitions, and post-merger integration and change management. Russell leads BCG's Women's Initiative for North America. Prior to joining BCG in 2001, Russell received her PhD in organic chemistry from Stanford University.

KUANG-TING TAI is a PhD student in the School of Public Affairs at Arizona State University. His primary research interests are local economic development, e-government, and open data. He is currently researching how local governments employ open-data policies to improve the level of transparency and to develop local economy.

ALFRED W. TATUM is interim dean and professor in the College of Education at the University of Illinois at Chicago. An expert on the literacy development of African American boys, he has authored more than fifty publications on the topic, including three books. Tatum also served on the board of directors at two major literacy organizations—the International Reading Association and the Literacy Research Association. Tatum was recently invited to participate in the National Summit on Educational Excellence and Opportunity for African American Males by the Department of Education as part of the White House Initiative on Educational Excellence for African Americans.

STEPHANIE TRUCHAN is a candidate for the master of urban planning and policy degree and a graduate assistant in the College of Urban Planning and Public Affairs at the University of Illinois at Chicago. Her master's focus is economic development, and she is particularly interested in land use law.

Truchan holds a bachelor of arts in English from Valparaiso University. She wrote regularly for Valparaiso University's student newspaper the *Torch* and on a rotation with the *Times of Northwest Indiana*.

DARRELL M. WEST is the vice president of governance studies and director of the Center for Technology Innovation at the Brookings Institution. He holds the Douglas Dillon Chair in Governance Studies. Previously, he was the John Hazen White Professor of Political Science and Public Policy and director of the Taubman Center for Public Policy at Brown University. West received the American Political Science Association's Don K. Price Award for best book on technology (for *Digital Government: Technology and Public Sector Performance*, 2005) and the American Political Science Association's Doris Graber Award for best book on political communications (for *Cross Talk: Citizens, Candidates, and the Media in a Presidential Campaign*, 1996).

HOWARD WIAL is the executive director of the Center for Urban Economic Development and associate professor of urban planning and policy at the University of Illinois at Chicago. He is also a nonresident senior fellow at the Brookings Institution. Wial's research focuses on manufacturing and urban and regional economic development. His previous experience includes being a resident fellow at Brookings, a research director of two think tanks, an economist at several U.S. government agencies, and a faculty member at multiple colleges and universities. He received his PhD in economics from the Massachusetts Institute of Technology and his JD from Yale Law School.

THE URBAN AGENDA

Metropolitan Resilience in a Time of Economic Turmoil
  Edited by Michael A. Pagano

Technology and the Resilience of Metropolitan Regions
  Edited by Michael A. Pagano

The University of Illinois Press
is a founding member of the
Association of American University Presses.

Composed in 10.5/13 Minion Pro
with Franklin Gothic display
by Jim Proefrock
at the University of Illinois Press
Manufactured by Cushing-Malloy, Inc.

University of Illinois Press
1325 South Oak Street
Champaign, IL 61820-6903
www.press.uillinois.edu